Readings in Literary Criticism 7
CRITICS ON BLAKE

Readings in Literary Criticism

CRITICS ON BLAKE

Readings in Literary Criticism

Edited by Judith O'Neill

University of Miami Press
Coral Gables, Florida

CONTENTS

ACKNOWLEDGEMENTS

We wish to thank the following for permission to reprint copyright material from the works listed below:

The Clarendon Press, Oxford (George Wingfield Digby's *Symbol and Image in William Blake*); Columbia University Press (Anthony F. Blunt's *Vision and Execution in Blake's Painting* in *The Art of William Blake*; Northrop Frye's *Blake's Treatment of the Archetype* in *English Institute Essays*; Edward B. Hungerford's *Blake's Albion* in *Shores of Darkness*; Milton O. Percival's *William Blake's Circle of Destiny*); Constable and Co. Ltd. (S. Foster Damon's *William Blake: His Philosophy and Symbols* and Arthur Symon's *William Blake*); J. M. Dent and Sons Ltd. (J. Middleton Murry's note in the facsimile edition of *Visions of the Daughters of Albion* and Joseph Wicksteed's *Blake's Vision of the Book of Job*); Doubleday and Co. Inc. (Martin Price's *Blake: Vision and Satire* in *To the Palace of Wisdom*); Faber and Faber Ltd. and Horizon Press (Herbert Read's *The Contrary Experience*); Holt Rinehart and Winston, Inc. (Mark Schorer's *The Decline of the Poet* in *William Blake: The Politics of Vision*); Johns Hopkins Press (Robert F. Gleckner's *Irony in Blake's 'Holy Thursday'* and John H. Sutherland's *Blake's Mental Traveller'*); Methuen and Co. Ltd. (T. S. Eliot's *Blake* in *The Sacred Wood*); Princeton University Press and the author (David V. Erdman's *Infinite London* in *Blake: Prophet Against Empire*); Tavistock Publications Ltd. and Pantheon Books (R. D. Laing's *The Divided Self*); University of Toronto Press (Peter Fisher's *The Valley of Vision*); Messrs. A. P. Watt and Son, Miss Anne Yeats and Mr. M. B. Yeats (W. B. Yeats's introduction to *The Poems of William Blake*).

Apart from his first poems, the *Poetical Sketches* published in 1783, Blake's poems were not printed in the usual way or sold to the general public like the works of most other poets. Starting with the *Songs of Innocence* of 1789, Blake produced each copy of his books of poems by his own method of illuminated printing. Sir Geoffrey Keynes, the distinguished editor of Blake, describes how it was done: 'The essence of the process was the integration of elaborate designs with text on a single etched copper-plate, which could be printed as a stereotype, the ink being transferred from the surface of the copper to the paper. But Blake was not content with making a plain print in black or coloured ink. He wished each page to have coloured designs interspersed with areas of text and to include a sprinkling of full-page designs without text. This he at first sought to achieve by printing in colours from the plate, so producing monotypes, or by making plain prints and then painting them with water-colour washes. Often he combined the two methods and always the process was laborious and slow. There was no "edition" in the ordinary sense; no two copies were exactly alike, and the number produced, as individual customers demanded them, was very small.' ('On Editing Blake', *English Studies Today*, 3rd Series, Edinburgh, 1964, p. 149.)

Blake then, never intended his poems to be read apart from his designs. If we see his poems only in a plain printed book, we are missing something essential that he meant us to enjoy. His text and designs are so closely related that each illumines and intensifies the meaning of the other. That is why it is worth making an effort (and even a journey) to see Blake's poems and designs together, either in their original form if you are fortunate enough to live near one of the museums where they are kept, or in the excellent facsimile volumes recently issued by the Blake Trust and available in many university libraries.

When you come to study the poems themselves, a few of them will already be familiar to you. 'The Lamb' and 'The Tyger', for example, have been so thoroughly anthologized that almost every school-child knows them. This points to one of the remarkable qualities of Blake's lyrics. They have a certain simplicity, a certain naive openness, that appeals to children as well as to adults. But the simplicity is deceptive. The poems are not as easy or as obvious as they look. Behind the song-like rhythms, the child-like questions and answers, the short lines and bright images, lies a subtle complexity of meaning that we only gradually learn to penetrate. In fact we never penetrate it completely and that is why the poems go on being a source of renewed pleasure all through life. 'The cistern contains: the fountain overflows.' Blake's poems go on overflowing. Their meaning can never be exactly and finally contained.

The best place to begin, although the obvious one, is with the *Songs of Innocence and Experience*, the Poems from the Notebook of 1793 (formerly known as the Rossetti Manuscript), the Poems from the Pickering Manuscript, and *The Marriage of Heaven and Hell*. In this collection of critical essays on Blake, I have tried to resist the temptation to offer the student a lot of detailed explications of these poems. Interesting and helpful though such interpretations often are, they would have spoiled the student's pleasure in discovering the richness of the poems for himself, either alone or, still more fruitfully, in a group with others. John H. Sutherland's classic essay on 'The Mental Traveller' will suggest a method of approach, a sensible and sensitive way of going about the study of a particular poem. Some good poems to start with are: 'I Asked a Thief', 'Ah! Sunflower', 'A Poison Tree', 'The Sick Rose', 'London', 'The Tyger', the two 'Holy Thursdays', and the two 'Nurse's Songs'. The critical essays in this book will help you most when you have already made a good attempt by yourself to read and unravel these poems. It is wise not to let even the best critic come between you and the initial experience of reading Blake's poems and of responding to them in your own way.

Once you move on from the shorter poems to the Prophetic Books you enter more difficult country and it is here that critics like Milton O. Percival, Northrop Frye and Peter Fisher will be of help in opening up Blake's key ideas and explaining his often puzzling use of myth and symbol. By reading the essays and extracts printed here, you will soon become familiar with the different *kinds* of current Blake criticism, and you can then follow up for yourself the fuller and more detailed studies by those critics you find most perceptive and convincing.

Cambridge, 1970   *Judith O'Neill*

Critics on Blake:
1803-1941

WILLIAM BLAKE: 1803
Three Years' Slumber

Now I may say to you what perhaps I should not dare to say to any one else: That I can alone carry on my visionary studies in London unannoy'd, & that I may converse with my friends in Eternity, See Visions, Dream Dreams & prophecy and speak Parables unobserv'd & at liberty from the Doubts of other Mortals; perhaps Doubts proceeding from Kindness, but Doubts are always pernicious, Especially when we Doubt our Friends. Christ is very decided on this Point: 'He who is Not With Me is Against Me.' There is no Medium or Middle state; & if a Man is the Enemy of my Spiritual Life while he pretends to be the Friend of my Corporeal, he is a Real Enemy—but the Man may be the friend of my Spiritual Life while he seem the Enemy of my Corporeal, but Not Vice Versa.

What is very pleasant, Every one who hears of my going to London again Applauds it as the only course for the interest of all concern'd in My Works, Observing that I ought not to be away from the opportunities London affords of seeing fine Pictures, and the various improvements in Works of Art going on in London.

But none can know the Spiritual Acts of my three years' Slumber on the banks of the Ocean, unless he has seen them in the Spirit, or unless he should read My long Poem descriptive of those Acts; for I have in these three years composed an immense number of verses on One Grand Theme, Similar to Homer's *Iliad* or Milton's *Paradise Lost*, the Persons & Machinery intirely new to the Inhabitants of Earth (some of the Persons Excepted). I have written this Poem[1] from immediate Dictation, twelve or sometimes twenty or thirty lines at a time, without Premeditation & even against my Will; the Time it has taken in writing was thus render'd Non Existent, & an immense Poem Exists which seems to be the Labour of a long Life, all produc'd without Labour or Study. I mention this to shew you what I think the Grand Reason of my being brought down here.

I have a thousand & ten thousand things to say to you. My heart is

---

[1] This poem is *Milton*, not *Jerusalem* as Cunningham assumed in 1830, see p. 17.

full of futurity. I perceive that the sore travel which has been given me
these three years leads to Glory and Honour. I rejoice & tremble:
'I am fearfully & wonderfully made.' I had been reading the cxxxix
Psalm a little before you Letter arrived. I take your advice. I see the
face of my Heavenly Father; he lays his Hand upon my Head & gives
a blessing to all my works; why should I be troubled? why should my
heart & flesh cry out? I will go on in the Strength of the Lord; through
Hell will I sing forth his Praises, that the Dragons of the Deep may
praise him, & that those who dwell in darkness & in the Sea Coasts
may be gather'd into his Kingdom. Excuse my, perhaps, too great
Enthusiasm. Please to accept of & give our Loves to Mrs Butts & your
amiable Family, & believe me to be,

Ever Yours Affectionately,
Will Blake

Letter to Thomas Butts, announcing Blake's intention to return to
London after three years at Felpham under the patronage of William
Hayley, April 25th, 1803. *Complete Works*, ed. G. Keynes, O.U.P.,
London, 1966, pp. 822–3. Blake's own spelling, etc., is preserved.

Both Poet and Painter

I hope that all our three years' trouble Ends in Good Luck at last &
shall be forgot by my affections & only remember'd by my Under-
standing; to be a Memento in time to come, & to speak to future
generations by a Sublime Allegory, which is now perfectly completed
into a Grand Poem. I may praise it, since I dare not pretend to be
any other than the Secretary; the Authors are in Eternity. I consider
it as the Grandest Poem that this World Contains. Allegory address'd
to the Intellectual powers, while it is altogether hidden from the
Corporeal Understanding, is My Definition of the Most Sublime
Poetry; it is also somewhat in the same manner defin'd by Plato.
This Poem shall, by Divine Assistance, be progressively Printed &
Ornamented with Prints & given to the Public. But of this work I
take care to say little to Mr H. [Hayley], since he is as much averse
to my poetry as he is to a Chapter in the Bible. He knows that I have
writ it, for I have shewn it to him, and he has read Part by his own
desire & has looked with sufficient contempt to inhance my opinion
of it. But I do not wish to irritate by seeming too obstinate in Poetic
pursuits. But if all the World should set their faces against This, I
have Orders to set my face like a flint (Ezekiel iiiC, 9v) against their
faces, & my forehead against their foreheads.

As to Mr H., I feel myself at liberty to say as follows upon this
ticklish subject: I regard Fashion in Poetry as little as I do in Paint-
ing; so, if both Poets & Painters should alternately dislike (but I know
the majority of them will not), I am not to regard it at all, but Mr H.
approves of My Designs as little as he does of my Poems, and I have

been forced to insist on his leaving me in both to my own Self Will; for I am determin'd to be no longer Pester'd with his Genteel Ignorance & Polite Disapprobation. I know myself both Poet & Painter, & it is not his affected Contempt that can move me to any thing but a more assiduous pursuit of both Arts. Indeed, by my late Firmness I have brought down his affected Loftiness, & he begins to think I have some Genius: as if Genius & Assurance were the same thing! but his imbecile attempts to depress Me only deserve Laughter. I say thus much to you, knowing that you will not make a bad use of it. But it is a Fact too true That, if I had only depended on Mortal Things, both myself & my Wife must have been Lost. I shall leave every one in This Country astonish'd at my Patience & Forbearance of Injuries upon Injuries; & I do assure you that, if I could have return'd to London a Month after my arrival here, I should have done so, but I was commanded by my Spiritual friends to bear all, to be silent, & to go thro' all without murmuring, &, in fine, hope, till my three years should be almost accomplish'd; at which time I was set at liberty to remonstrate against former conduct & to demand Justice & Truth; which I have done in so effectual a manner that my antagonist is silenc'd completely, & I have compell'd what should have been of freedom—My Just Right as an Artist & as a Man; & if any attempt should be made to refuse me this, I am inflexible & will relinquish any engagement of Designing at all, unless altogether left to my own Judgment, As you, My dear Friend, have always left me, for which I shall never cease to honour & respect you.

When we meet, I will perfectly describe to you my Conduct & the Conduct of others toward me, & you will see that I have labour'd hard indeed, & have been borne on angel's wings. Till we meet I beg of God our Saviour to be with you & me, & yours & mine. Pray give my & my wife's love to Mrs Butts & Family, & believe me to remain,

Yours in truth & sincerity,
Will Blake

Letter to Thomas Butts, written at Felpham, July 6th, 1803, *Ibid,* pp. 824-6.

1810   *The Outward Creation*

I assert for My Self that I do not behold the outward Creation & that to me it is hindrance & not Action; it is as the Dirt upon my feet, No part of Me. 'What,' it will be Question'd, 'When the Sun rises, do you not see a round disk of fire somewhat like a Guinea?' O no, no, I see an Innumerable company of the Heavenly host crying 'Holy, Holy, Holy is the Lord God Almighty.' I question not my Corporeal or Vegetative Eye any more than I would Question a Window concerning a Sight. I look thro' it & not with it.

'A Vision of the Last Judgment', from Blake's Note-Book for the year 1810, *Ibid,* p. 617.

BENJAMIN HEATH MALKIN: 1806

The Ancient Simplicity

He has made several irregular and unfinished attempts at poetry. He has dared to venture on the ancient simplicity; and feeling it in his own character and manners, has succeeded better than those, who have only seen it through a glass. His genius in this line assimilates more with the bold and careless freedom, peculiar to our writers at the latter end of the sixteenth and former part of the seventeenth century, than with the polished phraseology, and just but subdued thought of the eighteenth. . . .

[The Tyger] rises with the subject. It wears that garb of grandeur, which the idea of creation communicates to a mind of the higher order. Our bard, having brought the topic he descants on from warmer latitudes than his own, is justified in adopting an imagery, of almost oriental feature and complexion. . . .

Besides these lyric compositions, Mr Blake has given several specimens of blank verse. Here, as might be expected, his personifications are bold, his thoughts original, and his style of writing altogether epic in its structure. The unrestrained measure, however, which should warn the poet to restrain himself, has not infrequently betrayed him into so wild a pursuit of fancy, as to leave harmony unregarded, and to pass the line prescribed by criticism to the career of imagination. . . .

A Father's Memoirs of His Child, London, 1806. Extracts from the Dedicatory Letter, reprinted in Arthur Symons, William Blake, Constable and Company Ltd., London, 1907, pp. 317, 325, 327.

ROBERT HUNT: 1809

An Unfortunate Lunatic

If beside the stupid and mad-brained political projects of their rulers, the sane part of the people of England required fresh proof of the alarming increase of the effects of insanity, they will be too well convinced from its having lately spread into the hitherto sober region of Art. . . . When the ebullitions of a distempered brain are mistaken for the sallies of genius by those whose works have exhibited the soundest thinking in art, the malady has indeed attained a pernicious height, and it becomes a duty to endeavour to arrest its progress. Such is the case with the productions and admirers of WILLIAM BLAKE, an unfortunate lunatic, whose personal inoffensiveness secures him from confinement, and, consequently, of whom no public notice would have been taken, if he was not forced on the notice and animadversion of the Examiner, in having been held up to public admiration by many esteemed amateurs and professors as a genius in some respect original and legitimate. The praises which these gentlemen bestowed last year on this unfortunate man's illustrations of *Blair's Grave,* have, in feeding his vanity, stimulated him to publish his madness more largely, and thus again exposed him, if not to the derision, at least to the pity of the public. ...

The poor man fancies himself a great master, and has painted a few wretched pictures, some of which are unintelligible allegory, others an attempt at sober characters by caricature representation, and the whole 'blotted and blurred', and very badly drawn. These he calls an Exhibition, of which he has published a Catalogue, or rather a farrago of nonsense, unintelligibleness, and egregious vanity, the wild effusions of a distempered brain. ...

> 'Mr Blake's Exhibition', an anonymous article in *The Examiner,* no. 90, September 17th, 1809, pp. 605–6.

ROBERT SOUTHEY: 1811

A Decided Madman

July 24th, 1811. Late at C. Lamb's. Found a large party there. Southey had been with Blake, and admired both his designs and his poetic talents. At the same time he held him to be a decided madman. Blake, he said, spoke of his visions with the diffidence which is usual with such people, and did not seem to expect that he should be believed. He showed Southey a perfectly mad poem called *Jerusalem.* Oxford Street is in Jerusalem.

> Henry Crabb Robinson, *Diary, Reminiscences, and Correspondence,* ed. Thomas Sadler, 3 vols., London, 1869, vol. I, p. 338.

SAMUEL TAYLOR COLERIDGE: 1818

A Man of Genius

I have this morning been reading a strange publication—viz. Poems with very wild and interesting pictures, as the swathing, etched (I suppose) but it is said—printed and painted by the Author W. Blake. He is a man of Genius—and I apprehend, a Swedenborgian—certainly, a mystic emphatically. You perhaps smile at my calling another Poet, a Mystic; but verily I am in the very mire of common-place common-sense compared with Mr Blake, apo- or rather ana-calyptic Poet, and Painter!

> Letter to H. F. Cary, February 6th, 1818, *The Collected Letters of Samuel Taylor Coleridge,* ed. E. L. Griggs, vol. IV, 1815–1819, Clarendon Press, Oxford, 1959, pp. 833–4.

The 'Songs of Innocence and Experience'

N.B. I signifies, It gave me pleasure. I, still greater— I I, and

greater still. ⊙, in the highest degree, o, in the lowest. [Note by
S. T. C. o means that I am perplexed and have no opinion.]

Shepherd I. Spring I (last Stanza Ɪ). Holy Thursday ƖƖ. Laugh-
ing Song Ɪ. Nurse's Song I. The Divine Image ⊙. The Lamb Ɪ. The
little Black Boy ⊙: yea ⊙+⊙! Infant Joy ƖƖ. (N.b. for the 3 last
lines I should wish—When wilt thou smile, or—O smile, O smile!
I'll sing the while—For a Babe two days old does not, cannot *smile*
—and innocence and the very truth of Nature must go together.
Infancy is too holy a thing to be ornamented.)—Echoing Green I
(the figures Ɪ, and of the second leaf ƖƖ). The Cradle Song I. The
School boy ƖƖ, Night ⊙. On another's Sorrow I. A Dream ?—The
little Boy lost I (the drawing Ɪ). The little boy found I. The Blossom
o. The Chimney Sweeper o. The Voice of the ancient Bard o.

Introduction Ɪ. Earth's Answer Ɪ. Infant Sorrow I; The Clod and
the Pebble I. The Garden of Love Ɪ. The Fly I. The Tyger Ɪ. A
little Boy lost Ɪ. Holy Thursday I. P. 13, o. Nurse's Song ȯ. The
little girl lost and found (the ornaments most exquisite, the poem
I). Chimney Sweeper in the Snow o. To Tirzah—and The Poison
Tree I and yet o. A little girl lost o (I would have had it omitted—
not for the want of innocence in the poem, but from the too probable
want of it in many readers). London I. The sick Rose I. *The little
Vagabond*—Tho' I cannot approve altogether of this last poem and
have been inclined to think that the error which is most *likely* to beset
the scholars of Emanuel Swedenborg is that of utterly demerging the
tremendous incompatibilities with an evil will that arise out of the
essential Holiness of the abysmal Aseity in the Love of the eternal
Person—and thus giving temptation to weak minds to sink this Love
itself into *good nature,* & yet still I disapprove the mood of mind
in this wild poem so much less than I do the servile, blind worm,
wrap-rascal scurf-coat of FEAR of the *modern Saints* (whose whole
being is a Lie, to themselves as well as to their Brethren), that I
should laugh with good conscience in watching a Saint of the new
stamp, one of the Fixt Stars of our eleemosynary Advertisements,
groaning in wind-pipe! and with the whites of his Eyes upraised at
the *audacity* of this poem!—Anything rather than *this* degradation
of Humanity, and therein of the Incarnate Divinity.

Letter to C. A. Tulk, February 12th, 1818, *Ibid,* pp. 836–8.

CHARLES LAMB: 1824

A Most Extraordinary Man

Blake is a real name, I assure you, and a most extraordinary man,
if he be still living. He is the Robert [William] Blake, whose wild
designs accompany a splendid folio edition of the 'Night Thoughts',
which you may have seen.... He paints in water colours marvellous

strange pictures, visions of his brain, which he asserts that he has seen. They have great merit.... His poems have been sold hitherto only in Manuscript. I never read them; but a friend at my desire procured the 'Sweep Song'. There is one to a tiger, which I have heard recited, beginning—

> Tiger, Tiger, burning bright
> Thro' the desarts of the night

which is glorious, but alas! I have not the book; for the man is flown, whither I know not—to Hades or a Mad House. But I must look on him as one of the most extraordinary persons of the age....

Letter to Bernard Barton, May 15th, 1824, *Letters of Charles and Mary Lamb,* 1796–1820, edited by E. V. Lucas, Methuen, London, 1912, Letter 346, pp. 690–1.

HENRY CRABB ROBINSON: 1825–6

A Natural Sweetness and Gentility

December 10th, 1825. Dined with Aders. A very remarkable and interesting evening. The party at dinner, Blake the painter, and Linnell, also a painter.... Shall I call Blake artist, genius, mystic or madman? Probably he is all. I will put down without method what I can recollect of the conversation of this remarkable man. He has a most interesting appearance. He is now old (sixty-eight), pale, with a Socratic countenance, and an expression of great sweetness, though with something of languor about it except when animated, and then he has about him an air of inspiration ...

When he said 'my visions', it was in the ordinary unemphatic tone in which we speak of every-day matters. In the same tone he said repeatedly, 'the Spirit told me'. I took occasion to say, 'You express yourself as Socrates used to do. What resemblance do you suppose there is between your spirit and his?' 'The same as between our countenances.' He paused and added 'I was Socrates'—and then, as if correcting himself, said, 'a sort of brother. I must have had conversations with him. So I had with Jesus Christ. I have an obscure recollection of having been with both of them.' ... On my asking in what light he viewed the great question concerning the deity of Jesus Christ, he said, 'He is the only God. But then,' he added, 'and so am I and so are you.' ...

Blake said, 'I should be sorry if I had any earthly fame, for whatever natural glory a man has is so much taken from his spiritual glory. I wish to do nothing for profit. I wish to live for art. I want nothing whatever. I am quite happy.' Though he spoke of his happiness, he also alluded to past sufferings, and to suffering as necessary. 'There is suffering in heaven, for where there is the capacity of enjoyment, there is also the capacity of pain'....

I feel great admiration and respect for him. He is certainly a most amiable man—a good creature. And of his poetical and pictorial genius there is no doubt, I believe, in the mind of judges. Wordsworth and Lamb like his poems, and the Aderses his paintings. . . . There are a natural sweetness and gentility about Blake which are delightful.

December 24th. A call on Blake—my third interview. I read to him Wordsworth's incomparable ode [Intimations of Immortality] which he heartily enjoyed. But he repeated 'I fear Wordsworth loves nature and nature is the work of the Devil. The Devil is in us as far as we are nature'. The parts of Wordsworth's ode which Blake most enjoyed were the most obscure—at all events, those which I least like and comprehend.

February 18th, 1826. Called on Blake. . . . He warmly declared that all he knew is in the Bible. But he understands the Bible in its spiritual sense. . . . 'I write' he says, 'when commanded by the spirits, and the moment I have written I see the words fly about the room in all directions. It is then published and the spirits can read. My MS is of no further use. I have been tempted to burn my MSS, but my wife won't let me.' 'She is right' said I. . . .

Diary, Reminiscences, and Correspondence, ed. Thomas Sadler, 3 vols., London, 1869, vol. II, pp. 301–2, 304–7, 310, 316.

WILLIAM CAREY: 1827

Piously Cheerful

Blake has been allowed to exist in a penury which most artists—beings necessarily of a sensitive temperament—would deem intolerable. Pent, with his affectionate wife, in a close back-room in one of the Strand courts, his bed in one corner, his meagre dinner in another, a ricketty table holding his copper-plates in progress, his colours, books (among which his Bible, a Sessi Velutello's Dante, and Mr Carey's translation were at the top), his large drawings, sketches and MSS—his ankles frightfully swelled, his chest disordered, old age striding on, his wants increased, but not his miserable means and appliances: even yet was his eye undimmed, the fire of his imagination unquenched, and the preternatural, never-resting activity of his mind unflagging. He had not merely a calmly resigned, but a cheerful and mirthful countenance. . . . He took no thought for his life, what he should eat, or what he should drink; nor yet for his body, what he should put on; but had a fearless confidence in that Providence which had given him the vast range of the world for his recreation and delight.

Blake *died* last Monday! Died as he lived! Piously cheerful! talking calmly, and finally resigning himself to his eternal rest like an infant to its sleep. He has left *nothing* except some pictures, copper-plates, and his principal work, a Series of a hundred large Designs from Dante. . . .

The anonymous obituary notice on William Blake, *Literary Gazette,* no. 814, August 18th, 1827, pp. 540–1.

JOHN THOMAS SMITH: 1828
Enigmatically Curious

Much about this time [1784] Blake wrote many other songs to which he also composed tunes. These he would occasionally sing to his friends: and though, according to his confession, he was entirely unacquainted with the science of music, his ear was so good, that his tunes were sometimes most singularly beautiful, and were noted down by musical professors. As for his later poetry, if such it may be called, attached to his plates, though it was certainly in some parts enigmatically curious as to its application, yet it was not always wholly uninteresting; and I have unspeakable pleasure in being able to state, that though I admit he did not for the last forty years attend any place of Divine worship, yet he was not a Freethinker, as some invidious detractors have thought proper to assert, nor was he ever in any degree irreligious. Through life, his Bible was everything with him. . . .

Nollekens and His Times, London, 1828, vol. II, pp. 457–8.

A time will come when the numerous, though now very rare works of Blake (in consequence of his taking very few impressions from the plates before they were rubbed out to enable him to use them for other subjects) will be sought after with the most intense avidity. He was considered by Stothard and Flaxman (and will be by those of congenial minds, if we can reasonably expect such again) with the highest admiration. These artists allowed him their most unqualified praise, and were ever anxious to recommend him and his productions to the patron of the Arts; but, alas! they were not so sufficiently appreciated as to enable Blake, as every one could wish, to provide an independence for his surviving partner Kate, who adored his memory. . . .

A Book for a Rainy Day, London, 1845, pp. 81–2.

ALLAN CUNNINGHAM: 1830
'Jerusalem'

A production so exclusively wild was not allowed to make its appearance in any ordinary way: he thus announced it. 'After my three years' slumber on the banks of the ocean, I again display my giant forms to the public.' Of these designs there are no less than an hun-

B

dred; what their meaning is the artist has left unexplained. It seems of a religious, political and spiritual kind, and wanders from hell to heaven and from heaven to earth; now glancing into the distractions of our own days, and then making a transition to the antediluvians. The crowning defect is obscurity; meaning seems now and then about to dawn; you turn plate after plate and read motto after motto, in the hope of escaping from darkness into light. But the first might well be looked at last; the whole seems a riddle which no ingenuity can solve. Yet, if the work be looked at for form and effect rather than for meaning, many figures may be pronounced worthy of Michael Angelo. There is a wonderful freedom of attitude and position; men, spirits, gods, and angels, move with an ease which makes one lament that we know not wherefore they are put in motion.... He considered the *Jerusalem* to be his greatest work....

If we look at the man through his best and most intelligible works, we shall find that he who could produce the *Songs of Innocence and Experience*, the *Gates of Paradise*, and the *Inventions for Job*, was the possessor of very lofty faculties, with no common skill in art, and moreover that, both in thought and mode of treatment, he was a decided original. But should we, shutting our eyes to the merit of those works, determine to weigh his worth by his *Urizen*, his *Prophecies of Europe and America*, and his *Jerusalem*, our conclusion would be very unfavourable; we would say that, with much freedom of composition and boldness of posture, he was unmeaning, mystical, and extravagant, and that his original mode of working out his conceptions was little better than a brilliant way of animating absurdity.... Blake's misfortune was that of possessing this precious gift [imagination] in excess. His fancy overmastered him—until he at length confounded 'the mind's eye' with the corporeal organ, and dreamed himself out of the sympathies of actual life.

Lives of the Most Eminent British Painters, Sculptors and Architects, London, 1830, vol. II, pp. 158-9, 177-8.

ANON: LONDON UNIVERSITY MAGAZINE: 1830

An Early Appreciation

In our opinion, it was rather foolish of Mr Cunningham to attempt the life of so extraordinary a man as Blake, the peculiar character of whose mind he could no more comprehend, than he could produce rival works in either poetry or painting.... The public have only had a slight glimpse of the noble *Songs of Innocence and Experience*, by William Blake, but even that has laid open great beauties to its view. It is a curious circumstance, and well worthy the attention of all persons, that in this age of reason, Englishmen should have allowed two such men as Flaxman and Blake to pass from this life without evincing the smallest regard for them. Perhaps 'reason stumbles all night over bones of the dead' as Blake elegantly expressed it, and pays but small attention to real genius. . . .

Blake in his single person united all the grand combination of art and mind, poetry, music and painting. . . . As England is the least fettered by the minds of other nations, so Blake poured forth his effusions in his own grand style, copying no one . . . but breathing spirit and life into his works; and though shaping forms from the world of his creative and sportive imagination, yet he still remembered he was a moral as well as intellectual citizen of England, bound both to love and instruct her. . . . Painting is the flesh, poetry the bones, and music the nerves of Blake's work.

The figures surrounding and enclosing the poems produce fresh delight. They are equally tinged by a oetical idea, and though sometimes it is difficult to understand his wandering flights, yet the extraordinary ower developed in the handling of both arts astonish as well as delight. Here and there figures are introduced which, like the spirits in Macbeth, pass quickly from the sight; yet they every one of them have been well digested in the brain of a genius; and we should endeavour rather to unlock the prison-door in which we are placed, and gain an insight into his powerful mind than rail and scoff at him as a dreamer and madman.

For instance, Albion, with which the world is very little acquainted, seems the embodying of Blake's ideas on the present state of England; he viewed it not with the eyes of ordinary men, but contemplated it rather as a province of one grand man, in which diseases and crimes are continually engendered, and on this account he poured forth his poetical effusions somewhat in the style of Novalis, mourning over the crimes and errors of his dear country. . . . Horrid forms and visions pervade this Albion, for they were the only representatives, in his opinion, of the present state of mankind. No great genius wrote without having a plan, and so in this, a light is frequently thrown across the pictures, which partly discover the interior design of the Poet. We are perfectly aware of the present state of public opinion on this kind of man, but we know at the same time, that every genius has a certain end to perform and always runs before his contemporaries, and for that reason is not generally understood. This is our candid opinion with respect to Blake, but we hope that hereafter his merits will be more generally acknowledged. . . . We conclude . . . earnestly recommending the works of our author to the attention of the English nation, whereby their taste may be improved in the fine arts, as well as gratification derived from the perusal of his poetry.

'The Invention of William Blake, Painter and Poet', *London University Magazine*, vol. II, March 1830, pp. 318–23.

ALEXANDER GILCHRIST: 1863

The 'Songs of Innocence'

First of the Poems let me speak, harsh as seems their divorce from the Design which blends with them, forming warp and woof in one texture. It is like pulling up a daisy by the roots from the green sward out of which it springs. To me many years ago, first reading these weird Songs in their appropriate environment of equally spiritual form and hue, the effect was as that of an angelic voice singing to oaten pipe, such as Arcadians tell of; or, as if a spiritual magician were summoning before human eyes, and through a human medium, images and scenes of divine loveliness; and in the pauses of the strain, we seem to catch the rustling of angelic wings. The Golden Age independent of Space or Time, object of vague sighs and dreams from many generations of struggling humanity—an Eden such as childhood sees, is brought nearer than ever poet brought it before. For this poet was in assured possession of the Golden Age, within the chambers of his own mind. As we read, fugitive glimpses open, clear as brief, of our buried childhood, of an unseen world present, past, to come; we are endowed with new spiritual sight, with unwonted intuitions, bright visitants from finer realms of thought, which ever elude us, ever hover near. We encounter familiar objects, in unfamiliar transfigured aspects, simple expression and deep meanings, type and antitype. True, there are palpable irregularities, metrical licence, lapse of grammar, and even of orthography; but often the sweetest melody, most daring eloquence of rhythm, and what is more, appropriate rhythm. They are *unfinished* poems: yet would finish have bettered their bold and careless freedom? Would it not have brushed away the delicate bloom? that visible spontaneity, so rare and great a charm, the eloquent attribute of our old English Ballads, and of the early Songs of all nations. The most deceptively perfect wax-model is no substitute for the living flower. The form is, in these Songs, a transparent medium of the spiritual thought, not an opaque body....

An Undisciplined Artist

Both in his books and in conversation, Blake was a vehement *assertor;* very decisive and very obstinate in his opinions, when he had once taken them up. And he was impatient of control, or of a law in anything,—in his Art, in his opinions on morals, religion, or what not. If artists be divided into the disciplined and the undisciplined, he must fall under the latter category. To this, as well as to entire want of discipline in the literary art, was due much of the incoherence in his books and design; incoherence and wildness, which is another source of the general inference embodied by Wordsworth and Southey, who knew him only in his poems, when they described him as a man 'of great, but undoubtedly insane genius'. If for *insane* we read *undisciplined*, or ill-balanced, I think we shall hit the truth. . . .

> The Life of William Blake, 'Pictor Ignotus', With Selections from his Poems and Other Writings, 2 vols., London, 1863, vol. I, pp. 70–1, 329–30.

DANTE GABRIEL ROSSETTI: 1863

The 'Songs of Innocence and Experience'

The first series is incomparably the more beautiful of the two, being indeed almost flawless in essential respects; while in the second series, the five years intervening between the two had proved sufficient for obscurity and the darker mental phases of Blake's writing to set in and greatly mar its poetic value. This contrast is more especially evident in those pieces whose subjects tally in one and the other series. For instance, there can be no comparison between the first 'Chimney Sweeper', which touches with such perfect simplicity the true pathetic chord of its subject, and the second, tinged somewhat with the commonplaces, if also with the truths, of social discontents. . . .

> Note by Rossetti in Gilchrist's *Life of Blake*, London, 1863, vol. II, p. 25.

ALGERNON CHARLES SWINBURNE: 1868

The 'Marriage of Heaven and Hell'

. . . In 1790 Blake produced the greatest of all his books; a work indeed which we rank as about the greatest produced by the eighteenth century in the line of high poetry and spiritual speculation. The *Marriage of Heaven and Hell* gives us the high-water mark of his intellect. None of his lyrical writings show the same sustained strength and radiance of mind; none of his other works in verse or prose give more than a hint here and a trace there of the same harmonious and humorous power, of the same choice of eloquent words, the same noble command and liberal music of thought; small things he could often do perfectly, and great things often imperfectly; here for once he has written a book as perfect as his most faultless song, as great as his most imperfect rhapsody. His fire of spirit fills it from end to end; but never deforms the body, never singes the surface of the work, as too often in the still noble books of his later life. Across the flicker of flame, under the roll and roar of water, which seems to flash and resound throughout the poem, a stately music, shrill now as laughter and now again sonorous as a psalm, is audible through shifting notes and fitful metres of sound. The book swarms with heresies and eccentricities; every sentence bristles with some paradox, every page seethes with blind foam and surf of stormy doctrine; the humour is of that fierce grave sort, whose cool insanity of manner is more horrible and more obscure to the Philistine than any sharp edge of burlesque or glitter of irony; it is huge, swift, inexplicable; hardly laughable through its enormity of laughter, hardly significant through its condensation of meaning; but as true and thoughtful as the greatest humourist's. The variety and audacity of thoughts and words are incomparable: not less so their fervour and beauty. 'No bird soars too high if he soars with his own wings.' This proverb might serve as a motto to the book: it is one of many 'Proverbs of Hell', as forcible and as finished. . . .

'William Blake: A Critical Essay', 1868, *Complete Works of A. C. Swinburne*, ed. Gosse and Wise, Heinemann, London and New York, 1926, vol. 16, pp. 246–7.

W. B. YEATS: 1893

Blake's Ideas

. . . The essentials of the teaching of 'The Prophetic Books' can be best explained by extracts from the prose writings, for the language of the books themselves is exceedingly technical. 'God is in the lowest effects as well as in the highest causes,' he wrote on the margin of a copy of Lavater's 'Aphorisms'. 'For let it be remembered that creation is God descending according to the weakness of man. Our Lord is the word of God, and everything on earth is the word of God, and in its essence is God.' That portion of creation, however, which we can touch and see with our bodily senses is 'infected' with the power of Satan, one of whose names is 'Opacity'; whereas that other portion which we can touch and see with the spiritual senses, and which we call 'imagination', is truly 'the body of God', and the only reality; but we must struggle to really mount towards that imaginative world, and not allow ourselves to be deceived by 'memory' disguising itself as imagination. We thus mount by poetry, music, and art, which seek for ever 'to cast off all that is not inspiration', and 'the rotten rags of memory', and to become 'the divine members'. For this reason he says that Christ's apostles were all artists, and that 'Christianity is art', that 'the whole business of man is the arts', and that 'Israel delivered from Egypt is art delivered from nature and imitation'; and that we should all engage 'before the world in some mental pursuit'. We must take some portion of the kingdom of darkness, of the void in which we live, and by 'circumcizing away the indefinite' with a 'firm and determinate outline', make of that portion a 'tent of God', for we must always remember that God lives alone 'in minute particulars' in life made beautiful and graceful and vital by imaginative significance, and that all worthy things, all worthy deeds, all worthy thoughts, are works of art or of imagination. In so far as we do such works we drive the mortality, the infection, out of the things we touch and see, and make them exist for our spiritual senses—'the enlarged and numerous senses'; and beholding beauty and truth we see no more 'accident and chance', and the indefinite void 'and a last judgment' passes over us, and the world is consumed, for things are 'burnt up' 'when you cease to behold them'.

'Reason', or argument from the memory and from the sensations of the body, binds us to Satan and opacity, and is the only enemy of God. Sin awakens imagination because it is from emotion, and is therefore dearer to God than reason, which is wholly dead. Sin, however, must be avoided, because we are prisoners, and should keep the rules of our prison house, for 'you cannot have liberty in this world without what you call moral virtue, and you cannot have moral virtue without the subjection of that half of the human race who hate what you call moral virtue'. But let us recognize that these laws are but 'the laws of prudence', and do not let us call them 'the laws of God', for nothing is pleasing to God except the glad invention of beautiful and exalted things. He holds it better indeed for us to break all the commandments than to sink into a dead compliance. Better any form of imaginative evil—any lust or any hate—rather than an unimaginative virtue, for 'the human imagination alone' is 'the divine vision and fruition' 'in which man liveth eternally'. 'It is the human existence itself.' 'I care not whether a man is good or bad,' he makes Los, the 'eternal mind', say in *Jerusalem*; 'all that I care is whether he is a wise man or a fool. Go, put off holiness and put on intellect.' By intellect he means imagination. He who recognizes imagination for his God need trouble no more about the law, for he will do naught to injure his brother, for we love all which enters truly into our imagination, and by imagination must all life become one, for a man 'liveth not but in his brother's face', and by those 'loves and tears of brothers, sisters, sons, fathers, and friends, which if man ceases to behold he ceases to exist'....

Introduction to *The Poems of William Blake*, ed. W. B. Yeats, Laurence and Bullen and Charles Scribner's Sons, London and New York, 1893, pp. xxxv–xxxviii. This one-volume edition in the Muses' Library was published in the same year as the major three-volume edition of Blake's *Works*, edited by E. J. Ellis and W. B. Yeats with an extensive commentary on Blake's ideas and on the poems themselves.

ARTHUR SYMONS: 1907

The Ripening of Intuition

... The poetry of Blake is a poetry of the mind, abstract in substance, concrete in form; its passion is the passion of the imagination, its emotion is the emotion of thought, its beauty is the beauty of idea. When it is simplest, its simplicity is that of some 'infant joy' too young to have a name, or of some 'infant sorrow' brought aged out of eternity into the 'dangerous world', and there,

> Helpless, naked, piping loud,
> Like a fiend hid in a cloud.

There are no men and women in the world of Blake's poetry, only primal instincts and the energies of the imagination.

His work begins in the garden of Eden, or of the childhood of the world, and there is something in it of the naïveté of beasts: the lines gambol awkwardly, like young lambs. His utterance of the state of innocence has in it something of the grotesqueness of babies, and enchants the grown man, as they do. Humour exists unconscious of itself, in a kind of awed and open-eyed solemnity. He stammers into a speech of angels, as if just awakening out of Paradise. It is the primal instincts that speak first, before riper years have added wisdom to intuition. It is the supreme quality of this wisdom that it has never let go of intuition. It is as if intuition itself ripened. And so Blake goes through life with perfect mastery of the terms of existence, as they present themselves to him: 'perfectly happy, wanting nothing,' as he said, when he was old and poor; and able in each stage of life to express in art the corresponding stage of his own development. He is the only poet who has written the songs of childhood, of youth, of mature years, and of old age; and he died singing. . . .

William Blake, Archibald Constable and Company Ltd., London, 1907, pp. 66–7.

T. S. ELIOT: 1920

Blake

I

If one follows Blake's mind through the several stages of his poetic development it is impossible to regard him as a naïf, a wild man, a wild pet for the supercultivated. The strangeness is evaporated, the peculiarity is seen to be the peculiarity of all great poetry: something which is found (not everywhere) in Homer and Æschylus and Dante and Villon, and profound and concealed in the work of Shakespeare— and also in another form in Montaigne and in Spinoza. It is merely a peculiar honesty, which, in a world too frightened to be honest, is peculiarly terrifying. It is an honesty against which the whole world conspires, because it is unpleasant. Blake's poetry has the unpleasant- ness of great poetry. Nothing that can be called morbid or abnormal or perverse, none of the things which exemplify the sickness of an epoch or a fashion, have this quality; only those things which, by some extraordinary labour of simplification, exhibit the essential sickness or strength of the human soul. And this honesty never exists without great technical accomplishment. The question about Blake the man is the question of the circumstances that concurred to permit this honesty in his work, and what circumstances define its limitations. The favouring conditions probably include these two: that, being early apprenticed to a manual occupation, he was not compelled to acquire any other education in literature than he wanted, or to acquire it for any other reason than that he wanted it; and that, being a humble engraver, he had no journalistic-social career open to him.

There was, that is to say, nothing to distract him from his interests or to corrupt these interests: neither the ambitions of parents or wife, nor the standards of society, nor the temptations of success; nor was he exposed to imitation of himself or of anyone else. These circumstances—not his supposed inspired and untaught spontaneity —are what make him innocent. His early poems show what the poems of a boy of genius ought to show, immense power of assimilation. Such early poems are not, as usually supposed, crude attempts to do something beyond the boy's capacity; they are, in the case of a boy of real promise, more likely to be quite mature and successful attempts to do something small. So with Blake, his early poems are technically admirable, and their originality is in an occasional rhythm. The verse of *Edward III* deserves study. But his affection for certain Elizabethans is not so surprising as his affinity with the very best work of his own century. He is very like Collins, he is very eighteenth century. The poem 'Whether on Ida's shady brow' is eighteenth-century work; the movement, the weight of it, the syntax, the choice of words—

> The *languid* strings do scarcely move!
> The sound is *forc'd*, the notes are few!

this is contemporary with Gray and Collins, it is the poetry of a language which has undergone the discipline of prose. Blake up to twenty is decidedly a traditional.

Blake's beginnings as a poet, then, are as normal as the beginnings of Shakespeare. His method of composition, in his mature work, is exactly like that of other poets. He has an idea (a feeling, an image), he develops it by accretion or expansion, alters his verse often, and hesitates often over the final choice. The idea, of course, simply comes, but upon arrival it is subjected to prolonged manipulation. In the first phase Blake is concerned with verbal beauty; in the second he becomes the apparent naïf, really the mature intelligence. It is only when the ideas become more automatic, come more freely and are less manipulated, that we begin to suspect their origin, to suspect that they spring from a shallower source.

The *Songs of Innocence and of Experience,* and the poems from the Rossetti manuscript, are the poems of a man with a profound interest in human emotions, and a profound knowledge of them. The emotions are presented in an extremely simplified, abstract form. This form is one illustration of the eternal struggle of art against education, of the literary artist against the continuous deterioration of language.

It is important that the artist should be highly educated in his own art; but his education is one that is hindered rather than helped by the ordinary processes of society which constitute education for the ordinary man. For these processes consist largely in the acquisition of impersonal ideas which obscure what we really are and feel, what we really want, and what really excites our interest. It is of course not the actual information acquired, but the conformity which the accumulation of knowledge is apt to impose, that is harmful. Tennyson is a very fair example of a poet almost wholly encrusted with parasitic opinion, almost wholly merged into his environment. Blake, on the other hand, knew what interested him, and he therefore presents only the essential, only, in fact, what can be presented, and need not be explained. And because he was not distracted, or frightened, or occupied in anything but exact statement, he understood. He was naked, and saw man naked, and from the centre of his own crystal. To him there was no more reason why Swedenborg should be absurd than Locke. He accepted Swedenborg, and eventually rejected him, for reasons of his own. He approached everything with a mind unclouded by current opinions. There was nothing of the superior person about him. This makes him terrifying.

II

But if there was nothing to distract him from sincerity there were, on the other hand, the dangers to which the naked man is exposed. His philosophy, like his visions, like his insight, like his technique, was his own. And accordingly he was inclined to attach more importance to it than an artist should; this is what makes him eccentric, and makes him inclined to formlessness.

> But most through midnight streets I hear
> How the youthful harlot's curse
> Blasts the new-born infant's tear,
> And blights with plagues the marriage hearse,

is the naked vision;

> Love seeketh only self to please,
> To bind another to its delight,
> Joys in another's loss of ease,
> And builds a Hell in Heaven's despite,

is the naked observation; and *The Marriage of Heaven and Hell* is naked philosophy, presented. But Blake's occasional marriages of poetry and philosophy are not so felicitous.

> He who would do good to another must do it in Minute
> Particulars.

General Good is the plea of the scoundrel, hypocrite, and
    flatterer;
For Art and Science cannot exist but in minutely organized
    particulars. . . .

One feels that the form is not well chosen. The borrowed philosophy
of Dante and Lucretius is perhaps not so interesting, but it injures
their form less. Blake did not have that more Mediterranean gift of
form which knows how to borrow as Dante borrowed his theory of the
soul; he must needs create a philosophy as well as a poetry. A similar
formlessness attacks his draughtsmanship. The fault is most evident,
of course, in the longer poems—or rather, the poems in which struc-
ture is important. You cannot create a very large poem without intro-
ducing a more impersonal point of view, or splitting it up into various
personalities. But the weakness of the long poems is certainly not that
they are too visionary, too remote from the world. It is that Blake did
not see enough, became too much occupied with ideas.

We have the same respect for Blake's philosophy (and perhaps for
that of Samuel Butler) that we have for an ingenious piece of home-
made furniture: we admire the man who has put it together out of the
odds and ends about the house. England has produced a fair number
of these resourceful Robinson Crusoes; but we are not really so remote
from the Continent, or from our own past, as to be deprived of the
advantages of culture if we wish them.

We may speculate, for amusement, whether it would not have been
beneficial to the north of Europe generally, and to Britain in particular,
to have had a more continuous religious history. The local divinities
of Italy were not wholly exterminated by Christianity, and they were
not reduced to the dwarfish fate which fell upon our trolls and pixies.
The latter, with the major Saxon deities, were perhaps no great loss
in themselves, but they left an empty place; and perhaps our mytho-
logy was further impoverished by the divorce from Rome. Milton's
celestial and infernal regions are large but insufficiently furnished
apartments filled by heavy conversation; and one remarks about the
Puritan mythology an historical thinness. And about Blake's super-
natural territories, as about the supposed ideas that dwell there, we
cannot help commenting on a certain meanness of culture. They
illustrate the crankiness, the eccentricity, which frequently affects
writers outside of the Latin traditions, and which such a critic as
Arnold should certainly have rebuked. And they are not essential to
Blake's inspiration.

Blake was endowed with a capacity for considerable understanding
of human nature, with a remarkable and original sense of language
and the music of language, and a gift of hallucinated vision. Had these
been controlled by a respect for impersonal reason, for common sense,
for the objectivity of science, it would have been better for him.
What his genius required, and what it sadly lacked, was a framework

of accepted and traditional ideas which would have prevented him from indulging in a philosophy of his own, and concentrated his attention upon the problems of the poet. Confusion of thought, emotion, and vision is what we find in such a work as *Also Sprach Zarathustra*; it is eminently not a Latin virtue. The concentration resulting from a framework of mythology and theology and philosophy is one of the reasons why Dante is a classic, and Blake only a poet of genius. The fault is perhaps not with Blake himself, but with the environment which failed to provide what such a poet needed; perhaps the circumstances compelled him to fabricate, perhaps the poet required the philosopher and mythologist; although the conscious Blake may have been quite unconscious of the motives.

The Sacred Wood, Methuen, London, 1920, pp. 137–43.

JOSEPH WICKSTEED: 1924

'Vision of the Book of Job'

...Ever since his *Marriage of Heaven and Hell* and his *Songs of Experience* (both written more than thirty years before), he had been resolute to show a harmony in the sum of things which should explain the place of all that we falsely conceive as evil. He is essentially a system maker. 'I must Create a System or be enslav'd by another Man's,' he says. And his system was not framed to show that Hell does not exist, but that 'Hell is open'd to Heaven'. Hell being at worst a state of error not of sin.

With infinite sympathy, therefore, he sets out to reveal Job's error, and to explain how the man who seemed 'perfect' in life and thought was actually body and soul in Satan's power. 'Devils,' he says, 'are False Religions,' and he shows Job as a helpless victim of Satanic ideas, that could only be worked out of his soul by fiercest suffering and distress. And, when once we understand his method and accept his philosophical basis, Blake shows us with almost Shakespearean inevitableness the many-channelled course of error to despair. But despair is not for Blake the end. And if the first half of the book is great as tragedy—tragedy in which he remorselessly castigates the base ideas and ideals of his day—the latter half rises to that heavenly Comedy which lifts us into a paradise of enduring good. . . .

Job's error, according to Blake, was his boasted perfection itself. For the individual to be fortified with every outward and even inward good is not, as he supposes, to cut himself off from evil, but to cut himself off from an infinite good, which he can find only in a deep sense of imperfection and in the divine society of Man. This alone is Paradise, whether in earth or heaven. It is the difference between a tiny circle complete in itself and a small arc that only finds its completion in the circle of the universe. . . .

All good (and evil too, but evil is to him only a negation, or better still, a passage towards good) is inward and individual good; it is good to me or to you or to some particular person or creature. Salvation, happiness, beauty and, in a certain ultimate sense, God are brought to being in, and only in the individual soul. On the other hand, the individual, however noble, heroic or successful in himself, is the mere incarnation of Satan until he has lost and recovered his own good in the goodness of the Divine Humanity. And the essence of that Divine Humanity is love. No man has found *himself* until he has found so great a love of others that no act or thought of theirs can alienate them from him or make him wish for them other than the highest good. This is Jerusalem, Bride of Christ, the love of men as found in Man. . . .

Blake's Vision of the Book of Job, With Reproductions of the Illustrations, J. M. Dent and Sons Ltd., London, 1910, revised and enlarged edition 1924, pp. 65-6, 77-8, 82-3.

S. FOSTER DAMON: 1924

Three Songs of Experience

. . . 'The Tyger' deals with the immense problem of evil. . . . Blake could not consider Evil abstractly. His God was essentially personal; therefore Evil must be his Wrath. 'God out of Christ is a consuming fire,' he wrote elsewhere; and Crabb Robinson recorded that Blake said of Christ, 'He is the only God.'

The problem of 'The Tyger' is, quite simply, how to reconcile the Forgiveness of Sins (the Lamb) with the Punishment of Sins (the Tyger). So it is evident that the climax of 'The Tyger': 'Did he who made the Lamb make thee?' is not an exclamation of wonder, but a very real question, whose answer Blake was not sure of. The 27th Proverb of Hell distinctly states that 'The roaring of lions, the howling of wolves, the raging of the stormy sea, and the destructive sword are portions of eternity too great for the eye of man.'

Nevertheless Blake found some good in Wrath. 'The Wrath of the Lion is the Wisdom of God', and 'The Tygers of wrath are wiser than the Horses of instruction', are two other 'Proverbs of Hell'. . . .

A digression must be made here on the universal use of fire as a symbol of wrath. Blake, as we have seen, used it in his sentence, 'God out of Christ is a consuming fire'; and in *Urizen* he speaks of 'flames of eternal fury'. Boehme, in his fourth Epistle, wrote of 'the mystery of the wrath, or fire of God's anger'. In the *Faerie Queene* Spenser wrote: 'Wrath is a fire.' Milton also spoke of 'flames, the sign of wrath awaked'. Blake's association of fire with his Tyger (lines 1, 6, 8) was due to the old symbol.

Another very old symbol is that of the Forest. The Forest, in Blake, is the world of Experience, where the many sterile errors (dead trees) conceal the path and dim the light. . . .

With these two symbols fixed in our minds, we can see readily the answer to the question of the function of Wrath, concealed in the very first lines of the poem:

> Tyger, tyger, burning bright
> In the forests of the night.

Blake intends to suggest that the great purpose of Wrath is to consume Error, to annihilate those stubborn beliefs which cannot be removed by the tame 'horses of instruction'. . . .

The order of the lyric is typical of Blake. He shows the entire process of the tyger's creation. First the 'fire of his eyes' is gathered from the cosmos; then the heart is created, the feet forged, and ultimately the brain. . . . Blake describes the creation by a series of white-hot exclamations rather than by an elaborate description. The effect is one of an intense improvization; but an examination of the manuscripts shows at once that Blake made a great many corrections *during* the composition of the first draft. . . .

'Ah! Sunflower'. This is another of Blake's supreme poems. The music of it alone has been sufficient to make it unforgettable, though its meaning is concealed far beyond the casual reader's range of vision.

The sunflower, which is rooted in the earth, and whose face is supposed to follow the course of the sun, represented to Blake the man who is bound to the flesh, but who yearns after the liberty of Eternity.

The 'sweet golden clime where the traveller's [sun's] journey is done' is the west, which in all mythologies is the land of promise. To Blake it was essentially so, since there the Americas had recently established their liberty. A sexual significance is also given the poem by the second stanza. The liberty of the west was always, to Blake, a liberty of the body. Therefore the Virgins of both sexes aspire towards the west. But Blake (we need hardly warn the reader) meant this spiritually after all; since they 'arise from their graves' or bodies. Eternity can never be wholly attained in the flesh. Love is really only our guide there. . . .

'London'. This poem of concentrated wrath is directed against the corruption of civilization by the power of Reason, whose 'mind-forged manacles' have restricted every natural joy into a terrible agony. The street-cries of the chimney-sweeps are accusations against the Church; and the death-sigh of the soldier is a stain upon the State (how vividly Blake visualized that stain, as actually running in blood!). Love itself, when so bound, makes the marriage bed a disease-blighted hearse.

Everyone of us, at some moment of complete pessimism, has viewed the world in the same way, and has seen weakness and woe in every face. Blake's poem is not only a protest; it is a picture of a mental state....

William Blake: His Philosophy and Symbols, Constable and Company, Boston and London, 1924, pp. 276–8, 281–3.

JOHN MIDDLETON MURRY: 1932
'Visions of the Daughters of Albion'

... 'Good and evil are illusion; the body is not distinct from the soul, for that call'd Body is a portion of Soul discern'd by the five Senses, the chief inlets of Soul in this age.' That has always seemed to me a truly marvellous statement, incomparable for pregnancy and succinctness. Man is a unity, it says; but it says also that for man to gain knowledge of the nature of his own unity he must pass beyond the five senses that close him in and discover the total soul, of which the body is the portion discerned by the five senses. Blake's name for this total soul changed from time to time: he began by calling it The Poetic Genius or True Man. Later he called it the Eternal, or Universal Man. And as he developed with extraordinary subtlety the process of its re-creation 'in visionary forms dramatic', it became the regenerated Albion. But in all these successive elaborations the essential of the conception remains the same. It is the truth, which to Blake was blindingly obvious, that man is greater than he knows. He is, and must be, in Blake's peculiar sense, a 'spiritual' being. Of this spiritual being, Body as perceived by the senses is only a part; but it is an integral part. It is discerned by the senses, but the senses, if they are to perceive truly, and not merely 'through narrow chinks of the cavern', must perceive the Body as the 'spiritual' reality it is, not as the material reality it seems. Hence the manifest necessity of that 'improvement in sensual enjoyment', that seeing through not with the eye, hearing through not with the ear, which alone can lead us to the knowledge of the true Man, and of the true Universe in which he lives. By such cleansed and renewed perception we behold both the Infinite within and the Infinite without us; we pass, with the freedom of eternal beings, either inward or outward to Eternity.

This is, I believe, the core of Blake's revelation and his message. It is proclaimed on the title-page of *The Daughters of Albion*. 'The Eye sees more than the Heart knows'; that is, when the doors of vision have been cleansed. And the queer thing about this revelation is that it is so terribly, so appallingly obvious....

I think we need to be on our guard against those learned and well-meaning persons who would systematize Blake's symbols, and pin them down to hard and fast equivalents. No such translation is really possible. One is told, for instance, in *The Daughters of Albion*, that Bromion is Reason, Theotormon Desire, Oothoon Innocence: there is some truth in it, but not enough to be valuable. It would be truer to say that Bromion here represents the slave of the Law, and Oothoon the soul liberated from the Law, who seeks to communicate her freedom to others, but in vain.

However that may be, the important thing is to realize that for Blake enslavement to the Moral Law and the condition of confinement within the abyss of the five senses are generically the same condition. They are the same mutilation of the Eternal Man. Men and women are thus imprisoned because the doors of perception are not cleansed, because they are not aware of that which is greater than themselves seeking to inform them, and utter itself through them in new creativeness. The Cherub with the flaming sword still stands between them and the Tree of Life. They are unaware of their own infinity, and of the infinity of the universe. Therefore, lacking the power to apprehend the eternal source, which is also the immediate reality, of themselves and the world, they ensconce themselves in the seeming security of law, and seek to bind down life to a foregone pattern. This is that Tyranny which Blake hereafter will set before our imaginations under the grim figure of Urizen. . . .

Note by John Middleton Murry in the Facsimile Edition of *Visions of the Daughters of Albion*, J. M. Dent and Sons Ltd., London, 1932, pp. 13–14.

MILTON O. PERCIVAL: 1938

Blake's Philosophy

> . . . *I rest not from my great task,*
> *To open the Eternal Worlds, to open the immortal Eyes*
> *Of Man inwards into the Worlds of Thought, into Eternity*
> *Ever expanding in the Bosom of God, the Human Imagination.*
> *Jerusalem*, p. 5.

Of the many ironies which have gathered round the life and work of William Blake, two are pre-eminent. One is that he, the sanest and profoundest thinker among the poets of the romantic generation, was believed to be a madman. The other lies in the supposition that he read but little, that he put his philosophy together, Crusoe-like, from 'odds and ends about the house,' and that his great want was a 'framework of accepted and traditional ideas.' The former misconception requires no comment, for it is moribund; but the latter still prevails. Argument would be out of place in these introductory pages. I must content myself with a counter-statement. I predict, then, that when the evidence is in, it will be found that in the use of tradition Blake exceeded Milton and was second, if to anyone, only to Dante. To be sure, a great deal of the Blakean tradition might not be called 'accepted'. It certainly was not orthodox. But the Blakean heterodoxy was equally traditional with Dante's orthodoxy. The Orphic and Pythagorean tradition, Neoplatonism in the whole of its extent, the

Hermetic, kabbalistic, Gnostic, and alchemical writings, Erigena, Paracelsus, Boehme, and Swedenborg—here is a consistent body of tradition extending over nearly twenty-five hundred years. In the light of this tradition, not in the light of Christian orthodoxy, Blake read his Bible, weighing and deciding for himself, formulating a 'Bible of Hell'; for he was one in whose veins ran the dissidence of dissent and the protestantism of the Protestant religion. Anyone who undertakes to do Blake's reading after him will respect his prowess as a reader. Anyone who undertakes to evaluate his evaluations will, unless he is restrained by orthodoxy, respect his power as a thinker. When Blake in an impetuous moment, referred to himself as a 'mental prince', he uttered no more than sober truth.

So great was the impress of older thinking upon Blake's mind that it is difficult to fit him into the framework of his own time. Whether one thinks of that time as the declining Enlightenment or the rising Romantic Movement, he is an incongruous figure. The world of the Enlightenment was for him no less than a world ripe for a Last Judgment. In Blake's vision of the cosmic scheme the temporal wheel had almost come full circle. Nearly six thousand years ago the serpent of Natural Religion, not then recognized for what it was, had lured Albion out of Paradise. But now, at last, in the Natural Religion of the eighteenth century the error stood revealed in all its nakedness and turpitude. The round of error must either renew itself and swing over the long cycle once again, or be cast off, into the outer realm of possibility, to remain there as a memory and a warning. Which course would the cycle take? The Spectre in Blake made him painfully aware of error's power continually to renew. Where Babylon ends, Babylon might begin again. Eternal recurrence might be the pattern, as the Stoics said. But the prophet in him repudiated any such purposeless interpretation of experience. 'Time is the mercy of eternity', and its function, cruel and merciful at once, is to shape experience in such a way as to restore the wandering spirit to its source. Firmly persuaded that time had almost fulfilled its function, Blake rejoiced in visions of the Last Judgment and the ending of all things temporal. In the drumbeat of revolution in America and France, which to his forward-looking contemporaries heralded a Utopia to be reached over the road of perfectibility—the perfectibility of the natural man— Blake heard the doom of the natural man and the signal for the descent of the New Jerusalem out of heaven. In the rising Romantic Movement, he doubtless found some elements of the coming millennium yet his romanticism was different from any other. His primitivism owed more to Swedenborg than to the commoner romantic sources. His belief in progress, if he may be said to have entertained one, was simply in the Ring of Return. He hated Rousseau equally with Voltaire. With Shelley alone among the romantics could he have had any fundamental sympathy, if, indeed, fundamental sympathy

c

could be predicated of one who held the 'fatal and accursed' doctrine
of the goodness of the natural heart. He was really nearer to Plotinus
than to Shelley and nearer to certain Gnostic figures than to Plotinus.
He would have been more at home in the Alexandria of the third
century than he was in the London of his own time. The mystical
thinking, the millennial hopes, the heterodox interpretation of Christ's
mission, the spectre of natural religion—in short, nearly all the in-
gredients of Blake's thinking—were provided then. The manifold sys-
tems which went into the making of Blake's system either flourished in
that syncretistic time or had their roots there. If Blake is a modern
figure, it is because ancient thought can still be made significant.

And certainly Blake is a modern figure, so much so that to relegate
him to the ancient world seems like sheer paradox. He has more to
say to the present world than any other poet of his time, and more to
say about the issues of life than most poets of whatever time. He lived
in an era when modern problems were beginning to take shape. He
brought to bear upon them a mind capable of original and profound
interpretation of the cosmic drama, richly endowed with irony, shrewd-
ness, and common sense, undeceived by the solemn plausibilities of
the world, possessed, above all, of keen psychological insight. The
solutions which he reached are still cogent. His own age, which he
rejected except as it showed signs of regeneration, had the inestimable
value of acting as an irritant to his imagination.

> I turn my eyes to the Schools & Universities of Europe,
> And there behold the Loom of Locke, whose Woof rages dire
> Wash'd by the Water-wheels of Newton; black the cloth
> In heavy wreathes folds over every Nation.

Beholding this, he turned his eyes to the past and the future, so that
finally, after long contemplation, he was able to say: 'I see the past,
present and future existing all at once.' The myth corroborates this
assertion. It embraces the whole of human life, from the Fall to the
Last Judgment.

Blake's outline of the spiritual history of mankind is based upon the
Scriptures. The handicap implied by such restriction is not really as
great as might be supposed. Everything he knew, he told Crabb Robin-
son, was in the Bible. Yes, but the Bible can be read in a spiritual
sense, and one can find there, with a little ingenuity, whatever one is
looking for. Wide reading in philosophy had taught Blake very defi-
nitely what to look for, and several of his masters had taught him how
to find the most exotic fruit of allegory beneath the plainest leaves.
What a feeble obstacle the letter offered when Swedenborg and
Boehme and Philo of Alexandria searched their Scriptures, or when
the Neoplatonists subjected the ancient classics to new scrutiny! And
how Blake bettered the instruction! As the myth unrolls itself, especi-
ally in the *Four Zoas,* it weaves into its basically biblical pattern,

imagery and ideas from the poetic genius wherever that genius has devoted itself to things divine. The idea may have been suggested by Ovid, one of Blake's favourite authors. The *Metamorphoses* knits into one harmonious whole the myths of the ancient world from chaos and creation to the deification of Julius Caesar. This 'sublime and regular plan', as Bishop Warburton called it, he further describes as 'a popular history of Providence ... from the creation to his [Ovid's] own time, through the Egyptian, Phoenician, Greek and Roman histories'. Blake's plan, equally sublime and regular, purports to be a history of Providence as it has been manifested through the poetic genius in Egypt, Asia, Europe, and America, extending from the Creation to the Last Judgment.

It is obvious that Blake is one of those who have caught God's secret. Faith in such a secret might be called his birthright; his complete formulation of it does not come until fairly late. In a series of attempts, each more complex than the preceding one, he sought to formulate his faith into a system. The *Gates of Paradise*, which in its first state is early work, swings the cycle round with amazing rapidity, and yet the gist of the matter is contained in that sequence of sixteen plates. The early prophetic books carry the formulation into the field of myth, but even these were apparently regarded as inadequate, and the *Four Zoas* which followed immediately upon their completion, recounts the tale with much greater deliberation and complexity. This remains, indeed, the most 'sublime and regular' of all the versions. *Jerusalem,* however, tells the story once again from a different point of view, and *Milton,* though one of the most obscure of the prophetic writings, embodies the same doctrine. Turning from the pen to the graver, Blake embodied his own version of the Fall and the Redemption in his illustrations to *Paradise Lost* and *Paradise Regained.* Finally, in the Job illustrations, Job, the individual, passes over the same wheel of experience that Albion, the representative of mankind, had traversed in the *Four Zoas.* All these versions tally. The same key unlocks them all.

In view of all these presentations of the system, it is certainly ironical that Blake should be thought never to have achieved a system but to have lost himself in a maze of his own devising. Doubly ironical if he, whose abhorrence of the indefinite was so great that he made it a cornerstone of his philosophy, whose hero, Los, is forever hammering systems out of the hidden obscurity in which they lurk, who hated nothing so much as a polypus of incoherent roots, had become entangled in such a polypus himself. That he did not become so entangled, that on the contrary he had a system, a system as logical and coherent as any of the metaphysical systems formulated by the poets, [*William Blake's Circle of Destiny* undertakes to prove....]

'Introduction' to *William Blake's Circle of Destiny,* Columbia University Press, New York, 1938, pp. 3-5.

EDWARD B. HUNGERFORD: 1941

Blake's Use of Myth

... I have taken as my point of departure the dogmatic statement that Blake's dominating conviction was that man had departed from the guidance of God and that he should return to it. Scrutinizing the methods by which man might receive directly the guidance of God, Blake found the imagination to be an organ of the mind through which, in the form of symbolic visions, he could receive a direct apprehension of God's messages. These visions were, however, too personal to serve altogether as a means of communication to other persons. Believing that myths might also be interpreted as retaining symbolic representations of divine revelation, Blake attempted to clarify his own visions for his readers by equating them with parallel symbols which he found in the diverse myths of the world. The reader's difficulty lies in the fact that Blake's equations merely make darkness visible.

The trouble is that Blake, like the symbolists in mythological theory, was forced to suppose that myths had become seriously corrupted in their passage through time. Before they could be interpreted as symbols of a pristine divine revelation, it was necessary to divest them of all that was false, idolatrous and corrupt. In many cases an original symbol had come to be associated with merely historical events and personages of late periods in human history. The myths, therefore, had to be cleansed of all accretion before the original symbolic meaning could be recaptured. But in the process of divesture, Blake so mutilated the myths as to leave them barely recognizable. Their ordinary features, by which we might familiarly identify them, were obliterated. Moreover, in the effort to make them stand for a symbol of divine revelation, the meaning for which they stood had to be reduced to a vague and dim one—a faint theosophic promise of the regeneration of the soul through love, an intimation of immortality, or a promise of a redeemer and a judgment.... Blake's medium of expression proved to be an unfortunate one. The fault is somewhat mitigated by the fact that in the long run all the symbols resolve themselves into one and the same thing—their message is always basically the same: that man has departed from the guidance of God and that he should return to it. In effect one may actually ignore, without attempting very hard to understand, the whole immense apparatus in which the visionary poetry is communicated. When Blake has something to say, he says it very clearly, and it is usually worth listening to....

'Blake's Albion' in *Shores of Darkness*, Columbia University Press, New York, 1941, pp. 41–3.

Modern Critics on Blake

MARK SCHORER (1946)

Blake's Imagery

Blake's imagery demonstrates an analogous relationship between his
ideas and his art—the same doggedly independent ambitions, a reck-
less dependence on private associations or on associations without
references beyond the limits of the private 'system', and an original
and individual conception of the nature and functions of imagery.

The controlling fact that his imagery is the product of his vision, the
most private of all experiences, has two important consequences. At
their best, his images are fresh and illuminating and embody brilliant
insights, but at their worst, they are cloudy, vague, and perverse and
obscure his meaning. With the double development of the sense of a
prophetic function and of the idea of the uniqueness of all things, the
imagery more and more consistently operated as symbolism. These
two consequences are portions of the same general development, but
they may be treated separately.

The *Poetical Sketches,* in their imagery as in their diction, are
Blake's attempt to free himself from the conventional, and there is at
least as much of early seventeenth-century and of eighteenth-century
stock imagery as there is of the kind of original perceptions one as-
sociates with Blake in general. And among these 'flaming cars' and
'pale deaths' and 'deeps of Heaven' one comes across his extraordinary
innovations with a shock of discovery.

> ... Let thy west wind sleep on
> The lake; speak silence with thy glimmering eyes,
> And wash the dusk with silver—

one of the most astonishing images in this volume—really represents
a whole new way of *seeing* in poetry. It is a way that his visions enabled
him to explore, for he derived such boldness in his pictorializations
not from any traditional elements in poetry, but from his own early
visionary experiences. They supplied him, too, with ready-made pic-
tures. The lines in 'To Autumn'—

> ... joy, with pinions light, roves round
> The gardens, or sits singing in the trees—

may intend to comment on birds, but they are also reminiscent of
that childhood experience recounted by Gilchrist, when Blake saw 'a
tree filled with angels, bright angelic wings bespangling every bough
like stars'. It is impossible to tell what proportion of Blake's images
simply reproduce what he had beheld in vision, but that many of
them did, not a few of his pictures and drawings corroborate. A strik-
ing example is to be found in *The Four Zoas,* lines that duplicate
and explain a well-known picture:

> ...hovering high over his head
> Two winged immortal shapes, one standing at his feet
> Toward the East, one standing at his head toward the west,
> Their wings join'd in the Zenith over head....
> ...they bent over the dead corse like an arch,
> Pointed at top in highest heavens, of precious stones & pearl.
> Such is a Vision of All Beulah hov'ring over the Sleeper.

The content of Blake's vision is normally pastoral, with a Christian
emphasis. In *Poetical Sketches,* even ships are sheep, and stars are
already angels. From this primary inclination, Blake moves in two
directions. The imagery of pastoralism includes animals, but animals
are wild as well as mild, and the idyllic scene suggests its opposite.

> ...then the wolf rages wide,
> And the lion glares thro' the dun forest:
> The fleeces of our flocks are cover'd with
> Thy sacred dew: protect them.

Even now, that is, the vision darkens from idyllic reverie to observa-
tion of natural fact. The Christian concern has its other side too,
inevitably suggesting mortality and the melodrama of death. It is from
this concern, through his imitations of the Gothic fashion and the
graveyard poets, that Blake's apocalyptic imagery takes its start, and
with that, his images of a convulsive universe.

> The bell struck one, and shook the silent tower;
> The graves give up their dead

Such animation of earth suggests not only a lively nature in general,
but a nature mingling with man, and a nature, finally, that is domi-
nated by imagination. From all this Blake's particular and perpetual use
of the pathetic fallacy proceeds, for in his poems the device repre-
sents not merely a rhetorical inflation, but a view of the universe.[1]
Such a line as 'And the vale darkens at my pensive woe' gives the clue

---

[1] '... in their worlds (Darwin's and Blake's) *everything* feels; they use the
device not as a bestowal by man on nature, but as activity in a different
realm.'—Josephine Miles, *Pathetic Fallacy in the Nineteenth Century,* University
of California Press, 1942, p. 201. Miss Miles has inaugurated a valuable series
of studies on the relationship between verbal techniques and thought, of which
this is one. Her comments on Hopkins may be extended to include Blake and
should be examined by students of Blake's development.

to the real meaning of the imagery in the second stanza of 'Mad Song', where a dislocation of mind results in a dislocation of nature:

> Lo! to the vault
>   Of paved heaven,
> With sorrow fraught
>   My notes are driven:
> They strike the ear of night,
>   Make weep the eyes of day;
> They make mad the roaring winds,
>   And with tempests play.

The ease with which Blake animated the inanimate and mixed the animate with the inanimate resulted in some of his happiest pictorial effects, but it was also the particular ingredient in his talent that passed most rapidly out of his control and which then resulted in turgid and cloudy rhetoric.

The imagery of pastoral vision was apparently without such dangers for Blake. Here something, perhaps the simplification inherent in all idealizations, kept the imagery pure and clear. Consequently *Songs of Innocence* and *The Book of Thel*, which expand this single strain of imagery, are works without a single infelicity. The *Songs,* however, have a defect of resonance, a kind of attenuation which indicates that the visionary experience requires an infusion of something from nearer home. That infusion comes in *Songs of Experience,* poems that are correspondingly richer. The visionary experience never ceases to operate but now it collaborates beautifully with intellect.

> In what distant deeps or skies
> Burnt the fire of thine eyes?

That is, one would think, a Blakean vision in the most exact sense. Likewise, 'The Sun-flower':

> Where the Youth pined away with desire,
> And the pale Virgin shrouded in snow
> Arise from their graves, and aspire
> Where my Sun-flower wishes to go.

Yet in this last example, and throughout the *Songs of Experience,* there is a new intellectual element, observations on psychic friction and social pain that express themselves in the deliberately developed imagery of sex, and of commerce, industrialism, and science. These intellectual figurations lie outside the pastoral realm, and even outside the undiluted vision. They are Blake's most original contribution to the history of English poetry. They are poetry's debt to his determined independence—whole new fields of human experience relatively untouched by imagery before him;[2] and in these poems they

---

[2] It is interesting to note that Blake's entire range of industrial imagery has only a single line as predecessor in literature before him—Milton's 'Eyeless in Gaza, at the mill with slaves'.

sharpen his vision and weight it with meaning. Without this further element, he could not have written 'London', certainly not those particular lines which are among his greatest:

> And the hapless Soldier's sigh
> Runs in blood down Palace walls.

And without them he could not have conjured up his 'system'. When, in his prophetic poems, these elements enter into his visionary experience, the imagery is successful, and when they are neglected and the visionary experience operates alone, the imagery is unsuccessful. For it is the intellectual element that keeps our general human experience in view, and that maintains the balanced relationship between the world and the particularities of identity that is even more essential to art than it is to happiness.

This distinction may be tested, certainly in Blake's more ambitious images and in many of the more fleeting, by the extent of their associations, the degree to which the products of the private vision assimilate recognizable social or historical facts. Blake's many variations on 'a Cave, a Rock, a Tree deadly and poisonous', all traditional in themselves but capable of fresh figurations, as his use of them shows, are eminently successful. Besides their past histories in philosophy and religion, all of them have a genuinely literal significance: the darkness of the cave, the solidity or the impenetrability of the rock, and the tree's subtle and nearly ineradicable spread of roots as well as the production of fruit. Blake's use of such familiar images was thoughtful and often extremely ingenious, as when the tree, already associated with original sin, becomes an oak, and is further associated with the Druids, men of darkness.

So too such esoteric images as 'the Wicker Man of Scandinavia,' 'the Cities of the Salamandrine men,' and 'the Altars of Victims in Mexico' all have associative values that are effective for readers who do not assume that poetry involves no effort. And one may say the same for such more general images as 'Human Thought is crush'd beneath the iron hand of Power,' 'on my hands, death's iron gloves,' 'blue death in Albion's feet,' and 'Thought changed the infinite to a serpent, that which pitieth To a devouring flame.'

If we compare any of these with one of Blake's typical indiscretions in imagery, the difference is apparent. These lines from *The Four Zoas* will serve as an illustration:

> . . . they took the book of iron & placed above
> On clouds of death, & sang their songs, kneading the bread of Orc.
> Orc listen'd to the song, compell'd, hung'ring on the cold wind
> That swagg'd heavy with the accursed dough.

This dough serves no possible poetic purpose, for it suggests nothing but a weird confusion in the skies, wildly irrelevant both to nature and to mind, and rather foolish in its effect. It does serve to show, however, that vision is by no means wholly reliable as a pictorial source. Such excesses in his imagery are characteristic of the Prophetic poems, and they grow in number as Blake pursues his independent course. They are part and parcel of that earliest impulse to disrupt the universe, to penetrate the shell of matter by vision, to violate the mechanical. The impulse was capable of countless beautiful things, but when it was unguarded it often produced gross and bombastic follies.

The pathos of Blake's poetic development was that as he put more and more faith in vision, he felt less and less necessity to guard it. The result shows in another portion of the later imagery, his increasing pleasure in the poetic catalogue. This device is common in primitive poetry and in poetry imitative of primitive fashions. In Blake's early poems, even the early Prophecies, it had effective results, especially in his lists of animals and plants and their qualities. Later, when the device was employed merely to list proper names, of the twenty-seven churches and the innumerable cities, of the rivers and counties of England and the countries of Europe, of the multiple sons and daughters, it was turned into a perversely self-indulgent habit. These later catalogues may conceivably represent some grand panoramic spectacle in Blake's imagination, but they represent very little but an allegorical puzzle to the reader. Their exact meanings, if they had any, are nearly impossible to discover. Vision at its least successful became a matter of dark cryptography and mirror writing, of multiplication and amplification, as if Blake's content needed finally to be obscured and swollen to attain the grand Miltonic forms that were his ambition or even the exhalation of grandeur that he thought he detected in Macpherson.

Yet it would be a misrepresentation to let the matter stand there, Blake's aggressively independent imagination coming to such sad rest; for to the very end, when it allied itself with his equally aggressive social insights, it achieved imagery of the most penetrating kind. 'We were carried away in thousands,' he wrote in curiously modern lines that, commenting in general on human slavery and the toll of tyranny, yet had the objective core of comment on press gangs:

> We were carried away in thousands from London & in tens
> Of thousands from Westminster & Marybone, in ships clos'd up,
> Chain'd hand & foot, compell'd to fight under the iron whips
> Of our captains, fearing our officers more than the enemy.

In *Jerusalem*, too, are these lines, which present a general comment on the sources of human despair with a specific comment on absentee owners and the deadly monotony of piecework:

> . . . The captive in the mill of the stranger, sold for scanty hire.

They view their former life: they number moments over and
    over,
Stringing them on their remembrance as on a thread of sorrow.

In the same poem, his last, are many representations of that brilliant
historical perception into the complex catena of abstract science,
philosophy, techniques, and culture:

I turn my eyes to the Schools & Universities of Europe
And there behold the Loom of Locke, whose Woof rages dire,
Washed by the Water-wheels of Newton.

Blake's images are nearly always as surprising and as successful as
these when he achieves his poetic ambition, the implausible synthesis
of the visionary and the societal impulse. They are flat and unsuccess-
ful when his anarchism forgets its function as social analysis and shoots
off into the vision that is divorced from life. Yet that synthesis was
achieved through a private mythology, an elaborate symbolical struc-
ture that was not only the product of an anarchistic imagination but
was developed in order to elevate anarchy into public principle.

Blake was not, naturally, a symbolist in the sense of that term we
have derived from France; but all the elements that the *symbolistes*
isolated into a theory play a part in his more eclectic artistic purposes.
Even more than Yeats, he overlaid his symbolism with a system of
ideas, and he depended more than Yeats on explicit statement for the
operation of this system. Yet the formal dislocation of Blake's poems,
analogous to that derangement of the senses provided by his visionary
experiences, and the visionary experience itself, which assumes the
feasibility of discovering reality through the extrarational assertions of
the ego, even the final tendency of finding sacred the very disorder of
his mind—all these qualities relate Blake more closely to certain poets
of the late nineteenth century than to his contemporaries.

His visionary imagination seems to have contained a considerable
injection of what has been called 'empsychosis', a function that differs
'from imagination ... since the materials used for its products are
drawn, not from the senses, but from our invisible life of sentiment and
purpose'. A modification of this definition would describe the sym-
bolic imagination. It alters the process of metaphorical construction
by regarding the objects of sensuous experience as projections of emo-
tions and states of mind, and it constantly mingles matter and mind,
sense and spirit, by representing emotions and attitudes as objects, or,
less commonly, by representing objects as emotions and attitudes.

At its extreme, the tendency turns into surrealism. Blake differs
from both surrealists and symbolists in that his visions are not gener-
ally set down as 'free', the product of unanchored reverie or vagrant
association, but emerge in his poetry as forms of 'directed feeling',
and take their place in a construction that is basically logical rather
than hallucinatory, a product of the 'social ego' with a purpose ulti-

mately moral. His performance is not at all consistent. At one extreme he produces images such as that of the accursed dough swagging on the wind, which can only be described as surrealistic; at the other, his symbols stiffen into mere allegories not very different from Bunyan's, or Milton's of Sin and Death.

Between these extremes are the bulk of his figures, founded on a concept of the symbol as a means to knowledge and to power identical with the concept later developed by Mallarmé and Yeats. Yeats' comment, 'Then I draw myself up into the symbol and it seems as if I should know all if I could but banish such memories and find everything in the symbol,' expresses Blake's underlying ambition to turn art into ritual. 'If the Spectator could enter into these Images in his Imagination, approaching them on the Fiery Chariot of his Contemplative Thought, if he could Enter into Noah's Rainbow or into his bosom, or could make a Friend & Companion of one of these Images of wonder, which always intreats him to leave mortal things (as he must know), then would he arise from his Grave, then would he meet the Lord in the Air & then he would be happy. General Knowledge is Remote Knowledge; it is in Particulars that Wisdom consists & Happiness too.' The power of the symbol to transform matter and to expand mind lies in its representation of the uniqueness of every moment, the singularity of every thing, the identity of every individuality. Thus deviously eighteenth-century liberalism is transformed into an aesthetics.

The quality of Blake's symbols and the powers he ascribed to them are responsible for the strange character of his Prophecies, which are really forms of incantation. Yet he arrived at those symbols in the most mundane of literary ways. His evil gift in the *Poetical Sketches* is clearly also the evil gift of the poetry of his century—the facile device of personification; and from such devices spring even the grandest of his symbols. There is a process of foliation in the development of his imagery akin to that in Yeats, whose later poems, like Blake's, *seem* much more at variance with his early poems than they actually are. Thus, for example, one finds in the limp lines of *King Edward the Third* a blown-up description of 'golden London', the 'silver Thames', and an England 'overflowing with honey', whose very inflations Blake will presently press into the metaphysical purposes of symbolism. Here, too, in a song sung by a minstrel, liberty is an eagle, time is a sea, and the Trojan ancestors of the British (including 'Gothic Artists', no doubt) land 'in firm array upon the rocks Of Albion'. Here, as in 'Gwin', real human creatures sit in real caves, and in 'Fair Elinor' appears the grave—of such central importance in Blake's later symbolism—and it is at least as real as the graves in other eighteenth-century poems in the Gothic mood. The imagery of some primitivistic Eden-like time, when angels glittered in the sky for the edification of shepherds, occurs almost accidentally in 'Fresh from the dewy hill', and

the later concern with symbols of integration and unity finds its first
faint suggestion in the conventional lines of 'Love and harmony com-
bine'. Here, too, we may find the literary origins of Blake's gigantic
mythological creatures. Urizen, for example, emerges quite complete
in the personification of winter:

> O Winter! bar thine adamantine doors:
> The north is thine; there hast thou built thy dark
> Deep-founded habitation. Shake not thy roofs,
> Nor bend thy pillars with thine iron car.
>
> He hears me not, but o'er the yawning deep
> Rides heavy; his storms are unchain'd, sheathed
> In ribbed steel; I dare not lift mine eyes,
> For he hath rear'd his sceptre o'er the world.
>
> Lo! now the direful monster, whose skin clings
> To his strong bones, strides o'er the groaning rocks:
> He withers all in silence, and his hand
> Unclothes the earth, and freezes up frail life.
>
> He takes his seat upon the cliffs; the mariner
> Cries in vain. Poor little wretch! that deal'st
> With storms, till heaven smiles, and the monster
> Is driv'n yelling to his caves beneath mount Hecla.

The poem is worth quoting in its entirety because of its extraordinary
prophecy of what is to come, not only in the literal details of snow
and ice, dearth, desolation, steel and bones, cliffs and rocks, all of
which become the symbolical equipment of reason later, but more
particularly in the suggested narrative of a revolt from the proper
'place' ('The north is thine'), the chaos which follows, and the final
reachievement of a pastoral peace when the proper 'place' is once more
filled. This was to become the metaphor on which Blake's entire
mythology rested, and which was to give his Prophecies such structure
as they had.

The reader can follow the amplification and the specialization of
Blake's symbols from these humble sources, and it is possible to detect
in these sources the weakness as literary creations of those of his
symbols which are also characters. As these characters derive from the
popular device of personification, so also they suffer from the
eighteenth-century habit of generalization. His mythological figures
are totally devoid of the pictorial and particularized interest of the
mythological figures of Spenser and Milton and Keats, all of whom
we are made to feel as persons, or helped to visualize as creatures in a
pageant, or both.

It is true that Blake's ambitions were very different from those of
Spenser or Milton or Keats, but it is also true that the force of his
characters is not at all that of particularities but of abstractions. As he

personified the seasons in his first poems, so in his last he personified mercy, pity, peace, and love—and all other human qualities. He may have been, as various art critics have said, deficient in the descriptive imagination, but more than that, as his comments on Chaucer's characters and on his own kind of allegory suggest, he seems really to have submitted to that very tendency to generalize and idealize for which he never ceased to upbraid his contemporaries. He may have thought that he was expressing 'essences', yet the fact is that his 'essences' are at least as devoid of particularity as those fixed and final norms which the eighteenth century hoped to discover under the flux and shadows of temporal and local accident.

Among other poets who devised mythological characters, only those of Shelley are vaguer. Urizen, Urthona, Luvah, and Tharmas—how do we distinguish them? Are they not all the same loose-limbed giant in habiliments only so slightly different as not to be distinguishable at all except in wholly abstract terms? And is it not strange that an artist whose whole faith was in individuality produced hundreds of pictures filled with the same few recurrent physical types—the same old man, the same rather lumpish youth in his curious underwear, the gigantically muscled creature from Michelangelo, the rigid figure from Gothic tombs and columns (a very abstract model), and the airy females derived from a depraved popular art of Blake's own time? The point is that the individuality of these creations lies not in their rich diversity but in the outline that separates them from their backgrounds, and that outline, therefore, became the main item in Blake's aesthetic creed. This is not to deny his paintings any of their power or their beauty, but only to say what has always been known, that his was primarily a linear art.

Poetry, however, is a verbal art, without recourse to line, and the power of Blake's characters in the poems lies not in what they make us feel of themselves, as forms, but in their abstract utterances, and in the total meaning of which, taken together in the whole narrative pattern, they are the allegories. Does not Blake's individualism fail him, then, in the development of his symbols? In one sense, yes; but in another, no. For if it does not show itself in the creation of individuated forms, it does show itself in the value that Blake, as an individual, placed upon them. These creatures comprize a theogony, and they had real hypnagogic power for him, even when they do not compel us. His anarchism shows itself most clearly precisely here, in his eagerness to establish a private mythology and his willingness to submit his artistic fate to its characters, as some fervent laymen are willing to submit their fate to highly sectarian versions of God or to extremely fractional political groups. It is this that makes Blake's characters at once so flat and so terrible, so obscure and so portentous.

They are abstractions in a scheme designed to overcome abstraction, but in the poetry they retain the limitation that they transcend in the theory. Under Blake's protest against an isolated reason lies a framework of isolated reasoning that is not altered because he called it vision, and the result, prophecy.

From 'The Decline of the Poet', in *William Blake: The Politics of Vision*, New York, 1946, pp. 413–25. Copyright 1946 by Holt, Rinehart and Winston, Inc. Reprinted by permission of Holt, Rinehart and Winston, Inc.

Blake's Treatment of the Archetype

The reader of Blake soon becomes familiar with the words 'innocence' and 'experience'. The world of experience is the world that adults live in while they are awake. It is a very big world, and a lot of it seems to be dead, but still it makes its own kind of sense. When we stare at it, it stares unwinkingly back, and the changes that occur in it are, on the whole, orderly and predictable changes. This quality in the world that reassures us we call law. Sitting in the middle of the lawful world is the society of awakened adults. This society consists of individuals who apparently have agreed to put certain restraints on themselves. So we say that human society is also controlled by law. Law, then, is the basis both of reason and of society: without it there is no happiness, and our philosophers tell us that they really do not know which is more splendid, the law of the starry heavens outside us, or the moral law within. True, there was a time when we were children and took a different view of life. In childhood happiness seemed to be based, not on law and reason, but on love, protection, and peace. But we can see now that such a view of life was an illusion derived from an excess of economic security. As Isaac Watts says, in a song of innocence which is thought to have inspired Blake:

> Sleep, my babe; thy food and raiment,
> House and home, thy friends provide;
> All without thy care or payment:
> All thy wants are well supplied.

And after all, from the adult point of view, the child is not so innocent as he looks. He is actually a little bundle of anarchic will, whose desires take no account of either the social or the natural order. As he grows up and enters the world of law, his illegal desires can no longer be tolerated even by himself, and so they are driven underground into the world of the dream, to be joined there by new desires, mainly sexual in origin. In the dream, a blind, unreasoning, childish will is still at work revenging itself on experience and rearranging it in terms of desire. It is a great comfort to know that this world, in which we are compelled to spend about a third of our time, is unreal, and can never displace the world of experience in which reason predominates over passion, order over chaos, classical values over romantic ones, the solid over the gaseous, and the cool over the hot.

The world of law, stretching from the starry heavens to the moral conscience, is the domain of Urizen in Blake's symbolism. It sits on a volcano in which the rebellious Titan Orc, the spirit of passion, lies bound, writhing and struggling to get free. Each of these spirits is Satanic or devilish to the other. While we dream, Urizen, the principle of reality, is the censor, or, as Blake calls him, the accuser, a smug and grinning hypocrite, an impotent old man, the caricature that the child in us makes out of the adult world that thwarts him. But as long as we are awake, Orc, the lawless pleasure principle, is an evil dragon bound under the conscious world in chains, and we all hope he will stay there.

The dream world is, however, not quite securely bound: every so often it breaks loose and projects itself on society in the form of war. It seems odd that we should keep plunging with great relief into moral holidays of aggression in which robbery and murder become virtues instead of crimes. It almost suggests that keeping our desires in leash and seeing that others do likewise is a heavy and sooner or later an intolerable strain. On a still closer view, even the difference between war and law begins to blur. The social contract, which from a distance seems a reasonable effort of cooperation, looks closer up like an armed truce founded on passion, in which the real purpose of law is to defend by force what has been snatched in self-will. Plainly, we cannot settle the conflict of Orc and Urizen by siding with one against the other, still less by pretending that either of them is an illusion. We must look for a third factor in human life, one which meets the requirements of both the dream and the reality.

This third factor, called Los by Blake, might provisionally be called work, or constructive activity. All such work operates in the world of experience: it takes account of law and of our waking ideas of reality. Work takes the energy which is wasted in war or thwarted in dreams and sets it free to act in experience. And as work cultivates land and makes farms and gardens out of jungle and wilderness, as it domesticates animals and builds cities, it becomes increasingly obvious that work is the realization of a dream and that this dream is descended from the child's lost vision of a world where the environment is the home.

The worker, then, does not call the world of experience real because he perceives it out of a habit acquired from his ancestors: it is real to him only as the material cause of his work. And the world of dreams is not unreal, but the formal cause: it dictates the desirable human shape which the work assumes. Work, therefore, by realizing in experience the child's and the dreamer's worlds, indicates what there is about each that is genuinely innocent. When we say that a child is in the state of innocence, we do not mean that he is sinless or harmless, but that he is able to assume a coherence, a simplicity and a kindliness in the world that adults have lost and wish they could regain. When we dream, we are, whatever we put into the dream, revolting against experience and creating another world, usually one we like better. Whatever in childhood or the dream is delivered and realized by work is innocent; whatever is suppressed or distorted by experience becomes selfish or vicious. 'He who desires but acts not, breeds pestilence.'

Work begins by imposing a human form on nature, for 'Where man is not, nature is barren'. But in society work collides with the cycle of law and war. A few seize all its benefits and become idlers, the work of the rest is wasted in supporting them, and so work is perverted into drudgery. 'God made Man happy & Rich, but the Subtil made the innocent, Poor.' Neither idleness nor drudgery can be work: real work is the creative act of a free man, and wherever real work is going on it is humanizing society as well as nature. The work that, projected on nature, forms civilization, becomes, when projected on society, prophecy, a vision of complete human freedom and equality. Such a vision is a revolutionary force in human life, destroying all the social barriers founded on idleness and all the intellectual ones founded on ignorance.

So far we have spoken only of what seems naturally and humanly possible, of what can be accomplished by human nature. But if we confine the conception of work to what now seems possible, we are still judging the dream by the canons of waking reality. In other words, we have quite failed to distinguish work from law, Los from Urizen, and are back where we started. The real driving power of civilization and prophecy is not the mature mind's sophisticated and cautious adaptations of the child's or the dreamer's desires: it comes from the original and innocent form of those desires, with all their reckless disregard of the lessons of experience.

The creative root of civilization and prophecy can only be art, which deals not only with the possible, but with 'probable impossibilities'—it is interesting to see Blake quoting Aristotle's phrase in one of his marginalia. And just as the controlling idea of civilization is the humanizing of nature, and the controlling idea of prophecy the emancipation of man, so the controlling idea of art, the source of them both, must be the simultaneous vision of both. This is apocalypse, the complete transformation of both nature and human into the same form. 'Less than All cannot satisfy Man'; the child in us who cries for the moon will never stop crying until the moon is his plaything, until we are delivered from the tyranny of time, space, and death, from the remoteness of a gigantic nature and from our own weakness and selfishness. Man cannot be free until he is everywhere: at the centre of the universe, like the child, and at the circumference of the universe, like the dreamer. Such an apocalypse is entirely impossible under the conditions of experience that we know, and could only take place in the eternal and infinite context that is given it by religion. In fact, Blake's view of art could almost be defined as the attempt to realize

D

the religious vision in human society. Such religion has to be sharply
distinguished from all forms of religion which have been kidnapped
by the cycle of law and war, and have become capable only of rein-
forcing the social contract or of inspiring crusades.

When we say that the goal of human work can only be accomplished
in eternity, many people would infer that this involves renouncing all
practicable improvement of human status in favour of something
which by hypothesis, remains forever out of man's reach. We make
this inference because we confuse the eternal with the indefinite: we
are so possessed by the categories of time and space that we can hardly
think of eternity and infinity except as endless time and space, respec-
tively. But the home of time, so to speak, the only part of time that
man can live in, is now; and the home of space is here. In the world
of experience there is no such time as now; the present never quite
exists, but is hidden somewhere between a past that no longer exists
and a future that does not yet exist. The mature man does not know
where 'here' is: he can draw a circle around himself and say that
'here' is inside it, but he cannot locate anything except a 'there'.
In both time and space man is being continually excluded from his
own home. The dreamer, whose space is inside his mind, has a better
notion of where 'here' is, and the child, who is not yet fully conscious
of the iron chain of memory that binds his ego to time and space, still
has some capacity for living in the present. It is to this perspective
that man returns when his conception of 'reality' begins to acquire
some human meaning.

> The Sky is an immortal Tent built by the Sons of Los:
> And every Space that a Man views around his dwelling-
>   place
> Standing on his own roof or in his garden on a mount
> Of twenty-five cubits in height, such space is his Universe:
> And on its verge the Sun rises & sets, the Clouds bow
> To meet the flat Earth & the Sea in such an order'd Space:
> The Starry heavens reach no further, but here bend and
>   set
> On all sides, & the two Poles turn on their valves of
>   gold...

If the vision of innocence is taken out of its eternal and infinite
context, the real here and now, and put inside time, it becomes either
a myth of a Golden Age or a Paradise lost in the past, or a hope which
is yet to be attained in the future, or both. If it is put inside space, it
must be somewhere else, presumably in the sky. It is only these
temporal and spatial perversions of the innocent vision that really
do snatch it out of man's grasp. Because the innocent vision is so deep
down in human consciousness and is subject to so much distortion,
repression, and censorship, we naturally tend, when we project it on

the outer world, to put it as far off in time and space as we can get it. But what the artist has to reveal, as a guide for the work of civilization and prophecy, is the form of the world as it would be if we could live in it here and now.

Innocence and experience are the middle two of four possible states. The state of experience Blake calls Generation, and the state of innocence, the potentially creative world of dreams and childhood, Beulah. Beyond Beulah is Eden, the world of the apocalypse in which innocence and experience have become the same thing, and below Generation is Ulro, the world as it is when no work is being done, the world where dreams are impotent and waking life haphazard. Eden and Ulro are, respectively, Blake's heaven or unfallen world and his hell or fallen world. Eden is the world of the creator and the creature, Beulah the world of the lover and the beloved, Generation the world of the subject and the object, and Ulro the world of the ego and the enemy, or the obstacle. This is, of course, one world, looked at in four different ways. The four ways represent the four moods or states in which art is created: the apocalyptic mood of Eden, the idyllic mood of Beulah, the elegiac mood of Generation, and the satiric mood of Ulro. These four moods are the tonalities of Blake's expression; every poem of his regularly revolves on one of them.

For Blake the function of art is to reveal the human or intelligible form of the world, and it sees the other three states in relation to that form. This fact is the key to Blake's conception of imagery, the pattern of which I have tried to simplify by a table.

EXPERIENCE		CATEGORY	INNOCENCE	
Individual Form	*Collective Form*		*Collective Form*	*Individual Form*
sky-god (Nobodaddy)	aristocracy of gods	(1) Divine	human powers	incarnate God (Jesus)
a) leader and high priest (Caiaphas)	tyrants and victims	(2) Human	community	a) one man (Albion)
b) harlot (Rahab)				b) bride (Jerusalem)
dragon (Covering Cherub)	beasts of prey (tiger, leviathan)	(3) Animal	flock of sheep	one lamb (Bowlahoola)
tree of mystery	forest, wilderness (Entuthon Benython)	(4) Vegetable	garden or park (Allamanda)	tree of life
a) opaque furnace or brick kilns	a) city of destruction (Sodom, Babylon, Egypt)	(5) Mineral	city, temple (Golgonooza)	living stone
b) 'Stone of Night'	b) ruins, caves			
(not given)	salt lake or dead sea (Udan Adan)	(6) Chaotic	fourfold river of life	'Globule of Blood'

Let us take the word 'image' in its vulgar sense, which is good enough just now, of a verbal or pictorial replica of a physical object. For Blake the real form of the object is what he calls its 'human form'. In Ulro, the world with no human work in it, the mineral kingdom consists mainly of shapeless rocks lying around at random. When man comes into the world, he tries to make cities, buildings, roads, and sculptures out of this mineral kingdom. Such human artifacts therefore constitute the intelligible form of the mineral world, the mineral world as human desire would like to see it. Similarly, the 'natural' or unworked form of the vegetable world is a forest, a heath or a wilderness; its human and intelligible form is that of the garden, the grove, or the park, the last being the original meaning of the word Paradise. The natural form of the animal world consists of beasts of prey: its human form is a society of domesticated animals of which the flock of sheep is the most commonly employed symbol. The city, the garden and the sheepfold are thus the human forms of the mineral, vegetable, and animal king-doms, respectively. Blake calls these archetypes Golgonooza, Alla-manda, and Bowlahoola, and identifies them with the head, heart, and bowels of the total human form. Below the world of solid substance is a chaotic or liquid world, and the human form of that is the river or circulating body of fresh water.

Each of these human forms has a contrasting counterpart in Ulro, the world of undeveloped nature and regressive humanity. To the city which is the home of the soul or City of God, the fallen world opposes the city of destruction which is doomed through the breakdown of work described by Ezekiel in a passage quoted by Blake as 'pride, fullness of bread and abundance of idleness'. Against the image of the sheep in the pasture, we have the image of the forest inhabited by menacing beasts like the famous tiger, the blasted heath or waste land full of monsters, or the desert with its fiery serpents. To the river which is the water of life the fallen world opposes the image of the devouring sea and the dragons and leviathans in its depths. Blake usually calls the fallen city Babylon, the forest Entuthon Benython, and the dead sea or salt lake Udan Adan. Labyrinths and mazes are the only patterns of Ulro; images of highways and paths made straight belong to the world informed with intelligence.

The essential principle of the fallen world appears to be discreteness or opacity. Whatever we see in it we see as a self-enclosed entity, un-like all others. When we say that two things are identical, we mean that they are very similar; in other words 'identity' is a meaningless word in ordinary experience. Hence in Ulro, and even in Generation, all classes or societies are aggregates of similar but separate indivi-duals. But when man builds houses out of stones, and cities out of houses, it becomes clear the the real or intelligible form of a thing includes its relation to its environment as well as its self-contained existence. This environment is its own larger 'human form'. The stones that make a city do not cease to be stones, but they cease to be separate stones: their purpose, shape, and function is identical with that of the city as a whole. In the human world, as in the work of art, the individual thing is there, and the total form which gives it meaning is there: what has vanished is the shapeless collection or mass of similar things. This is what Blake means when he says that in the apocalypse all human forms are 'identified'. The same is true of the effect of work on human society. In a completely human society man would not lose his individuality, but he would lose his separate and isolated ego, what Blake calls his Self-hood. The prophetic vision of freedom and equality thus cannot stop at the Generation level of a Utopia, which means an orderly molecular aggregate of individuals existing in some future time. Such a vision does not capture, though it may adumbrate, the real form of society, which can only be a larger human body. This means literally the body of one man, though not of a separate man.

Everywhere in the human world we find that the Ulro distinction between the singular and the plural has broken down. The real form of human society is the body of one man; the flock of sheep is the body of one lamb; the garden is the body of one tree, the so-called tree of life. The city is the body of one building or temple, a house of many mansions, and the building itself is the body of one stone, a glowing and fiery precious stone, the unfallen stone of alchemy which assimilates everything else to itself, Blake's grain of sand which contains the world.

The second great principle of Ulro is the principle of hierarchy or degree which produces the great chain of being. In the human world there is no chain of being: all aspects of existence are equal as well as identical. The one man is also the one lamb, and the body and blood of the animal form are the bread and wine which are the human forms of the vegetable world. The tree of life is the upright vertebrate form of man; the living stone, the glowing transparent furnace, is the furnace of heart and lungs and bowels in the animal body. The river of life is the blood that circulates within that body. Eden, which according to Blake was a city as well as a garden, had a fourfold river, but no sea, for the river remained inside Paradise, which was the body of one man. England is an island in the sea, like St John's Patmos; the human form of England is Atlantis, the island which has replaced the sea. Again, where there is no longer any difference between society and the individual, there can hardly be any difference between society and marriage or between a home and a wife or child. Hence Jerusalem in Blake is 'A City, yet a Woman', and at the same time the vision of innocent human society.

On the analogy of the chain of being, it is natural for man to invent an imaginary category of gods above him, and he usually locates them in what is above him in space, that is, the sky. The more developed society is, the more clearly man realizes that a society of gods would have to be, like the society of man, the body of one God. Eventually he realizes that the intelligible forms of man and of whatever is above man on the chain of being must be identical. The identity of God and man is for Blake the whole of Christianity: the adoration of a super-human God he calls natural religion, because the source of it is remote and unconquered nature. In other words, the superhuman God is the deified accuser or censor of waking experience, whose function it is to discourage further work. Blake calls this God Nobodaddy, and curses and reviles him so much that some have inferred that he was inspired by an obscure psychological compulsion to attack the Fatherhood of God. Blake is doing nothing of the kind, as a glance at the last plate of *Jerusalem* will soon show: he is merely insisting that man cannot approach the superhuman aspect of God except through Christ, the God who is Man. If man attempts to approach the Father directly, as Milton, for instance, does in a few unlucky passages in *Paradise Lost* all he will ever get is Nobodaddy. Theologically, the only unusual feature of Blake is not his attitude to the person of the Father, but his use of what is technically known as pre-existence: the doctrine that the humanity of Christ is co-eternal with his divinity.

There is nothing in the Ulro world corresponding to the identity of the individual and the total form in the unfallen one. But natural religion, being a parody of real religion, often develops a set of individual symbols corresponding to the lamb, the tree of life, the glowing stone, and the rest. This consolidation of Ulro symbols Blake calls Druidism. Man progresses toward a free and equal community, and regresses toward tyranny; and as the human form of the community is Christ, the one God who is one Man, so the human form of tyranny is the isolated hero or inscrutable leader with his back to an aggregate of followers, or the priest of a veiled temple with an imaginary sky-god supposed to be behind the veil. The Biblical prototypes of this leader and priest are Moses and Aaron. Against the tree of life we have what Blake calls the tree of mystery, the barren fig tree, the dead tree of the cross, Adam's tree of knowledge, with its forbidden fruit corresponding to the fruits of healing on the tree of life. Against the fiery precious stone, the bodily form in which John saw God 'like a jasper and a sardine stone', we have the furnace, the prison of heat without light which is the form of the opaque warm-blooded body in the world of frustration, or the stone of Druidical sacrifice like the one that Hardy associates with Tess. Against the animal body of the lamb, we have the figure that Blake calls, after Ezekiel, the Covering Cherub, who represents a great many things, the unreal world of gods, human tyranny and exploitation, and the remoteness of the sky, but whose animal form is that of the serpent or dragon wrapped around the forbidden tree. The dragon, being both monstrous and fictitious, is the best animal representative of the bogies inspired by human inertia: the Book of Revelation calls it 'the beast that was, and is not, and yet is'.

Once we have understood Blake's scheme of imagery, we have broken the back of one of the main obstacles to reading the prophecies: the difficulty is grasping their narrative structure. Narrative is normally the first thing we look for in trying to read a long poem, but Blake's poems are presented as a series of engraved plates, and the mental process of following a narrative sequence is, especially in the later poems, subordinated to a process of comprehending an inter-related pattern of images and ideas. The plate in Blake's epics has a function rather similar to that of the stanza with its final alexandrine in *The Faerie Queene:* it brings the narrative to a full stop and forces the reader to try to build up from the narrative his own reconstruction of the author's meaning. Blake thinks almost entirely in terms of two narrative structures. One of these is the narrative of history, the cycle of law and war, the conflict of Orc and Urizen, which in itself has no end and no point and may be called the tragic or historical vision of life. The other is the comic vision of the apocalypse or work of Los, the clarification of the mind which enables one to grasp the human form of the world. But the latter is not concerned with temporal sequence and is consequently not so much a real narrative as a dialectic.

The tragic narrative is the story of how the dream world escapes into experience and is gradually imprisoned by experience. This is the main theme of heroic or romantic poetry and is represented in Blake by Orc. Orc is first shown us, in the 'Preludium' to *America,* as the libido of the dream, a boy lusting for a dim maternal figure and bitterly hating an old man who keeps him in chains. Then we see him as the conquering hero of romance, killing dragons and sea monsters, ridding the barren land of its impotent aged kings, freeing imprisoned women, and giving new hope to men. Finally we see him subside into the world of darkness again from whence he emerged, as the world of law slowly recovers its balance. His rise and decline has the rotary movement of the solar and seasonal cycles, and like them is a part of the legal machinery of nature.

Blake has a strong moral objection to all heroic poetry that does not see heroism in its proper tragic context, and even when it does he is suspicious of it. For him the whole conception of $\kappa\lambda\acute{\epsilon}\alpha$ $\alpha\nu\varsigma\epsilon\hat{\omega}\nu$ as being in itself, without regard to the larger consequences of brave deeds, a legitimate theme for poetry, has been completely outmoded. It has been outmoded, for one thing, by Christianity, which has brought to the theme of the heroic act a radically new conception of what a hero is, and what an act is. The true hero is the man who, whether as thinker, fighter, artist, martyr, or ordinary worker, helps in achieving the apocalyptic vision of art; and an act is anything that has a real relation to that achievement. Events such as the battle of Agincourt or the

retreat from Moscow are not really heroic, because they are not really
acts: they are part of the purposeless warfare of the state of nature
and are not progressing towards a better kind of humanity. So Blake
is interested in Orc only when his heroism appears to coincide with
something of potentially apocalyptic importance, like the French or
American revolutions.

For the rest, he keeps Orc strictly subordinated to his main theme
of the progressive work of Los, the source of which is found in pro-
phetic scriptures, especially, of course, the Bible. Comprehensive as
his view of art is, Blake does not exactly say that the Bible is a work
of art: he says 'The Old & New Testaments are the Great Code of
Art'. The Bible tells the artist what the function of art is and what his
creative powers are trying to accomplish. Apart from its historical and
political applications, Blake's symbolism is almost entirely Biblical in
origin, and the subordination of the heroic Orc theme to the apoca-
lyptic Los theme follows the Biblical pattern.

The tragic vision of life has the rhythm of the individual's organic
cycle: it rises in the middle and declines at the end. The apocalyptic
theme turns the tragic vision inside out. The tragedy comes in the
middle, with the eclipse of the innocent vision, and the story ends
with the re-establishment of the vision. Blake's major myth thus breaks
into two parts, a Genesis and an Exodus. The first part accounts for
the existence of the world of experience in terms of the myths of
creation and fall. Blake sees no difference between creation and fall,
between establishing the Ulro world and placing man in it. How man
fell out of a city and garden is told twice in Genesis, once of Adam and
once of Israel—Israel, who corresponds to Albion in Blake's symbo-
lism, being both a community and a single man. The Book of Genesis
ends with Israel in Egypt, the city of destruction. In the Book of
Exodus we find the state of experience described in a comprehensive
body of Ulro symbols. There is the fallen civilization of Egypt, des-
troyed by the plagues which its own tyranny has raised, the devouring
sea, the desert with its fiery serpents, the leader and the priest, the
invisible sky god who confirms their despotic power, and the labyrin-
thine wanderings of a people who have nothing but law and are unable
to work. Society has been reduced to a frightened rabble following a
leader who obviously has no notion of where he is going. In front of
it is the Promised Land with its milk and honey, but all the people can
see are enemies, giants, and mysterious terrors. From there on the story
splits in two. The histories go on with the Orc or heroic narrative of
how the Israelites conquered Canaan and proceeded to run through
another cycle from bondage in Egypt to bondage in Babylon. But
in the prophecies, as they advance from social criticism to apocalyptic,
the Promised Land is the city and garden that all human effort is try-
ing to reach, and its conqueror can only be the Messiah or true form
of man.

The New Testament has the same structure as the Old. In the life of Jesus the story of the Exodus is repeated. Jesus is carried off to Egypt by a father whose name is Joseph, Herod corresponds to Pharaoh, and the massacre of the innocents to the attempt to exterminate the Hebrew children. The organizing of Christianity around twelve disciples corresponds to the organizing of the religion of Israel among twelve tribes, the forty days wandering of Jesus in the desert to the forty years of Israel, the crucifixion to the lifting of the brazen serpent on the pole, and the resurrection to the invasion of Canaan by Joshua, who has the same name as Jesus. From there on the New Testament splits into a historical section describing the beginning of a new Christian cycle, which is reaching its Babylonian phase in Blake's own time, and a prophetic section, the Book of Revelation, which deals with what it describes, in a phrase which has fascinated so many apocalyptic thinkers from Joachim of Floris to Blake, as the 'everlasting gospel', the story of Jesus told not historically as an event in the past, but visually as a real presence.

The characters of Blake's poems, Orc, Los, Urizen, Vala, and the rest, take shape in accordance with Blake's idea of the real act. No word in the language contains a greater etymological lie than the word 'individual'. The so-called undivided man is a battleground of conflicting forces, and the appearance of consistency in his behaviour derives from the force that usually takes the lead. To get at the real elements of human character, one needs to get past the individual into the dramatis personae that make up his behaviour. Blake's analysis of the individual shows a good many parallels with more recent analyses, especially those of Freud and Jung. The scheme of the Four Zoas is strikingly Freudian, and the contrast of the Orc and Los themes in Blake is very like the contrast between Jung's early book on the libido and his later study of the symbols of individuation. Jung's anima and persona are closely analogous to Blake's emanation and spectre and his counsellor and shadow seem to have some relation to Blake's Los and Spectre of Urthona.

But a therapeutic approach will still relate any such analysis primarily to the individual. In Blake anything that is a significant act of individual behaviour is also a significant act of social behaviour. Orc, the libido, produces revolution in society: Vala, the elusive anima, produces the social code of *Frauendienst*; Urizen, the moral censor, produces the religion of the externalized God. 'We who dwell on Earth can do nothing of ourselves,' says Blake: 'everything is conducted by Spirits.' Man performs no act as an individual: all his acts are determined by an inner force which is also a social and historical force, and they derive their significance from their relation to the total human act, the restoration of the innocent world. John Doe does nothing as John Doe: he eats and sleeps in the spirit of Orc the Polypus: he obeys laws in the spirit of Urizen the conscience; he loses his temper in the spirit of Tharmas the destroyer; and he dies in the spirit of Satan the death-impulse.

Furthermore, as the goal of life is the humanization of nature, there is a profound similarity between human and natural behaviour, which in the apocalypse becomes identity. It is a glimmering of this fact that has produced the god, the personalized aspect of nature, and a belief in gods gradually builds the sense of an omnipotent personal community out of nature. As long as these gods remain on the other side of nature, they are merely the shadows of superstition: when they are seen to be the real elements of human life as well, we have discovered the key to all symbolism in art. Blake's Tharmas, the 'id' of the individual and the stampeding mob of society, is also the god of the sea, Poseidon the earth-shaker. His connection with the sea is not founded on resemblance or association, but, like the storm scene in *King Lear,* on an ultimate identity of human rage and natural tempest.

In the opening plates of *Jerusalem* Blake has left us a poignant account of one such struggle of contending forces within himself, between his creative powers and his egocentric will. He saw the Industrial Revolution and the great political and cultural changes that came with it, and he realized that something profoundly new and disquieting was coming into the world, something with unlimited possibilities for good or for evil, which it would tax all his powers to interpret. And so his natural desire to make his living as an engraver and a figure in society collided with an overwhelming impulse to tell the whole poetic truth about what he saw. The latter force won, and dictated its terms accordingly. He was not allowed to worry about his audience. He revised, but was not allowed to decorate or stylize, only to say what had to be said. He was not allowed the double talk of the sophisticated poet, who can address several levels of readers at once by using familiar conceptions ambiguously. Nothing was allowed him but a terrifying concentration of his powers of utterance.

What finally emerged, out of one of the hottest poetic crucibles of modern times, was a poetry which consisted almost entirely in the articulation of archetypes. By an archetype I mean an element in a work of literature, whether a character, an image, a narrative formula, or an idea, which can be assimilated to a larger unifying category. The existence of such a category depends on the existence of a unified conception of art. Blake began his prophecies with a powerfully integrated theory of the nature, structure, function, and meaning of art, and all the symbolic units of his poetry, his moods, his images, his narratives and his characters, form archetypes of that theory. Given his premises about art, everything he does logically follows. His premises may be wrong, but there are two things which may make us hesitate to call them absurd. One is their comprehensiveness and consistency: if the Bible is the code of art, Blake seems to provide something of a code of modern art, both in his structure of symbols and in his range of ideas. The other is their relationship to earlier traditions of criticism. Theories of poetry and of archetypes seem to belong to criticism rather than to poetry itself, and when I speak of Blake's treatment of the archetype I imply that Blake is a poet of unique interest to critics like ourselves. The Biblical origin of his symbolism and his apocalyptic theory of perception have a great deal in common with the theory of anagoge which underlies the poetry of Dante, the main structure of which survived through the Renaissance at least as late as Milton. Blake had the same creative powers as other great poets, but he made a very unusual effort to drag them up to consciousness, and to do deliberately what most poets prefer to do instinctively. It is possible that what impelled him to do this was the breakdown of a tradition of criticism which could have answered a very important question. Blake did not need the answer, but we do.

The question relates to the application of Blake's archetypes to the criticism of poetry as a whole. Pure research is, up to a point, a co-ordinated and systematic form of study, and the question arises whether *general criticism* could also acquire a systematic form. In other words, is criticism a mere aggregate of research and comment and generalization, or is it, considered as a whole, an intelligible structure of knowledge? If the latter, there must be a quality in litera- ture which enables it to be so, an order of words corresponding to the order of nature which makes the natural sciences intelligible. If criti- cism is more than aggregated commentary, literature must be some- what more than an aggregate of poems and plays and novels: it must possess some kind of total form which criticism can in some measure grasp and expound.

It is on this question that the possibility of literary archetypes de- pends. If there is no total structure of literature, and no intelligible form to criticism as a whole, then there is no such thing as an arche- type. The only organizing principle so far discovered in literature is chronology, and consequently all our larger critical categories are con- cerned with sources and direct transmission. But every student of literature has, whether consciously or not, picked up thousands of resemblances, analogies, and parallels in his reading where there is no question of direct transmission. If there are no archetypes, then these must be merely private associations, and the connections among them must be arbitrary and fanciful. But if criticism makes sense, and litera- ture makes sense, then the mental processes of the cultivated reader may be found to make sense too.

The difficulty of a 'private mythology' is not peculiar to Blake: every poet has a private mythology, his own formation of symbols. His mythology is a cross-section of his life, and the critic, like the bio- grapher, has the job of making sure that what was private to the poet shall be public to everyone else. But, having no theory of archetypes, we do not know how to proceed. Blake supplies us with a few leading principles which may guide us in analyzing the symbolic formation of poets and isolating the archetypal elements in them. Out of such a study the structure of literature may slowly begin to emerge, and criticism, in interpreting that structure, may take its rightful place among the major disciplines of modern thought. There is, of course, the possibility that the study of Blake is a long and tortuous blind alley, but those who are able to use Blake's symbols as a calculus for all their criticism will not be much inclined to consider it.

The question that we have just tried to answer, however, is not the one that the student of Blake most frequently meets. The latter question runs in effect: you may show that Blake had one of the most powerful minds in the modern world, that his thought is staggeringly comprehensive and consistent, that his insight was profound, his mood exalted, and his usefulness to critics unlimited. But surely all this profits a poet nothing if he does not preserve the hieratic decorum of conventional poetic utterance. And how are we to evaluate an utterance which is now lucid epigram and now a mere clashing of symbols, now disciplined and lovely verse and now a rush of prosy gabble? Whatever it is, is it really poetry or really great and good poetry? Well, probably not, in terms of what criticism now knows, or thinks it knows, about the canons of beauty and the form of literary expression.

Othello was merely a bloody farce in terms of what the learned and acute Thomas Rymer knew about drama. Rymer was perfectly right in his own terms; he is like the people who say that Blake was mad. One cannot refute them; one merely loses interest in their conception of sanity. And critics may be as right about Blake as Rymer was about Shakespeare, and still be just as wrong. We do not yet know whether literature and criticism are forms or aggregates: we know almost nothing about archetypes or about any of the great critical problems connected with them. In Dante's day critics did know something about the symbols of the Bible, but we have made little effort to recover that knowledge. We do not know very much even about genres: we do not know whether Blake's 'prophecy' form is a real genre or not, and we certainly do not know how to treat it if it is. I leave the question of Blake's language in more competent hands, but after all, even the poets are only beginning to assimilate contemporary speech, and when the speech of *Jerusalem* becomes so blunt and colloquial that Blake himself calls it prosaic, do critics really know whether it is too prosaic to be poetic, or even whether such an antithesis exists at all? I may be speaking only of myself, for criticism today is full of confident value-judgments, on Blake and on everyone else, implying a complete understanding of all such mysteries. But I wonder if these are really critical judgments, or if they are merely the aberrations of the history of taste. I suspect that a long course of patient and detailed study lies ahead of us before we really know much about the critical problems which the study of Blake raises, and which have to be reckoned with in making any value-judgment on him. Then we shall understand the poets, including Blake, much better, and I am not concerned with what the results of that better understanding will be.

English Institute Essays, 1950, ed. Alan S. Downer, Columbia University Press, New York, 1951, pp. 170–96.

DAVID V. ERDMAN (1954; 1969)

Infinite London: The *Songs of Experience* in their Historical Setting

Relatively little of the considerable and increasing store of commentary on the *Songs of Experience* deals with their historical matrix; yet it would be pedantic here ... to go beyond calling attention to the particular setting of some of their major themes. Though immeasurably closer than the prophecies to Blake's ideal of an art that rises above its age 'perfect and eternal', these great lyrics soar up from a particular moment of history. The fused brilliance of 'London' and 'The Tyger', the sharp, poignant symbolism of 'The Garden of Love', 'Infant Sorrow', and many another 'indignant page' were forged in the heat of the Year One of Equality (September 1792 to 1793) and tempered in the 'grey-brow'd snows' of Antijacobin alarms and proclamations.

The fearful symmetry of the period in its cosmic implications produced Blake's boldest Oothoonian question, 'The Tyger'.... The recurrent negative theme in the *Songs* is the mental bondage of Antijacobinism, manifest not in the windy caves of Parliament or the archetypal howlings of Albion's Guardians but in the lives of children and youth forced into harlotry and soldiery and apprentice slavery by the bone-bending, mind-chaining oppressions of priest and king. In *Europe* and *America* Blake sketches a panoramic view of the youth of England and their parents walking heavy and mustering for slaughter while their minds are choked by volumes of fog which pour down from 'Infinite London's awful spires' and from the palace walls and 'cast a dreadful cold Even on rational things beneath'. In *Songs of Experience* he takes us into the dismal streets and into schoolroom and chapel to see the effects of Empire on the human 'flowers of London town'. He describes, in 'The Human Abstract', the growth of the evil tree which is gallows, cross, and the abstract Mystery that hides the facts of war. The roots of this oak or upas tree of perverted Druidism are watered by the selfish tears of Mercy, Pity, and Peace:

> Pity would be no more,
> If we did not make somebody Poor;
> And Mercy no more could be,
> If all were as happy as we;

> And mutual fear brings peace;
> Till the selfish loves increase.

This tree grows 'in the Human brain', planted there by priest and king, who use the virtuousness of pity as an excuse for poverty and who define peace as an armistice of fear—and thus 'promote war'.[1]

It is instructive to note that ideas like these were widely propagated in the latter part of 1792 by an Association for Preserving Liberty and Property against Republicans and Levellers—expressly to persuade 'the minds of ignorant men' that all causes of discontent were either inescapable or wholly imaginary, and to prepare these minds for the eventuality of England's being 'dragged into a French war'.[2]

These pamphleteers were in favour of the mutual fear and 'military policy' that temporarily bring peace and ultimately bring war.[3] And they bluntly defended the inequality that supports pity and mercy. Both the Bible and 'experience', they said, tell us that 'society cannot exist without a class of poor'. Consequently it is our duty to teach the poor that their sufferings are necessary and natural and not to be remedied by laws or constitutional changes—that it is in fact the object of our maligned and 'most excellent Government to alleviate poverty' by 'poor laws, work-houses and hospitals'.[4] Blake's suspicion that 'Churches, Hospitals, Castles, Palaces' are the 'nets & gins & traps' of the 'Code of War'[5] is confirmed by these anti-levellers: 'Every step ... which can be taken to bind man to man, order to order, the lower to the higher, the poor to the rich, is now a more peculiar duty; and if there are any means to prevent the spreading of dangerous and delusive principles, they must be sought for in education. [Hence the need for] Foundation Schools, Hospitals, Parish Schools, and Sunday Schools.'[6]

In 'The Schoolboy' Blake is concerned not simply about the constraint of the classroom in summer weather but about the moral

---

[1] 'The Human Abstract' and draft called 'The Human Image' (*N.* 107) in which the 'mystery' is discussed that 'The priest promotes war & the soldier peace'. Cf. Marg. to Watson, iv: E601/K384. [E = *The Poetry and Prose of William Blake*, ed. Erdman, Garden City, 1965; K= *The Complete Writings of William Blake*, ed. Keynes, London, 1966]. For a discussion of the relations of these poems and of the internal evidence for an early date for 'A Divine Image' (confirmed now by script) see Robert F. Gleckner, 'William Blake and "The Human Abstract"', *PMLA*, LXXVI (1961), 373–9.

[2] I quote from *Politics ... Reflections on the Present State of Affairs*, by a Lover of His Country, Edinburgh, 1792. For the Association, see *London Chronicle*, Nov. 27-29, 1792.

[3] *Politics*. On the one hand, peace is 'an object of desire' most effectually approached, we are told, by 'a military policy' and increased armaments; on the other hand, if our 'great empire is insulted by the impudent memorials of a set of plunderers' (the rulers of France) war will be 'necessary and unavoidable'.

[4] William Vincent, *A Discourse to the People*, London, 1792.

[5] *Song of Los*: K246.

[6] Vincent.

defeatism forced upon 'the little ones' who are compelled to 'spend the day In sighing and dismay'. And in the poem that follows, Blake's Bard has a contrary educational programme:

> Youth of delight, come hither,
> And see the opening morn,
> Image of truth new born.

No use to 'stumble all night over bones of the dead'.[7]

Blake's counterargument is that if there were not 'so many children poor' there would be no need for institutions and moral code—and no ignorant men for sale to the fat fed hireling. Poverty appalls the mind, making youth sufficiently docile to be led 'to slaughter houses' and beauty sufficiently desperate to be 'bought & sold ... for a bit of bread' (N. 107). There can be no vital bond of man to man in such 'a land of Poverty!' Starvation demonstrates the absurdity of the anti-vice campaign, for the church remains spiritually and physically a cold barn, to which the Little Vagabond rightly prefers the warm tavern.[8] The harlot's curse will weave Old England's winding sheet, and ultimately the raging desire for bread will undermine the whole misery-built London of spire and palace.

Boston's Angel asked, 'What crawling villain preaches abstinence & wraps himself In fat of lambs?' The chimney sweep, a 'little black thing among the snow', answers that it is

> God & Priest & King,
> Who wrap themselves up in our misery [deleted reading]
> And because I am happy & dance & sing
> They think they have done me no injury. (N. 103)

King, priest, god, and parents do not reckon the revolutionary potential in the multitude they are stripping naked. Yet even the sheep puts forth 'a threat'ning horn' against the tithing priest (N. 109). As for the chimney sweeper, his father and mother have turned a happy boy into a symbol of death. Once a year he still does dance and sing—on May Day, when London streets are given to the sweeps and milkmaids

---

[7] 'The Schoolboy' and 'The Voice of the Ancient Bard', first published among *Songs of Innocence*; cf. second Proverb of Hell in *M.H.H.*: E35/K150.

[8] A curious 'mark of weakness' appears in Blake's own publication. In etching the 'Vagabond', Blake bowdlerized the fourth line, changing 'makes all go to hell' to 'will never do well', thereby introducing a bad rhyme and an ambiguity rather than defy the moral code of the Vice Society. The first notebook draft (N. 105) reads:

> Dear Mother Dear Mother the church is cold
> But the alehouse is healthy & pleasant & warm
> Besides I can tell where I am us'd well,
> Such usage in heaven makes all go to hell.

Even as published, the 'audacity' and 'mood' of this wild poem disturbed *Coleridge* in 1818. *Collected Letters*, ed. E. L. Griggs, Oxford, 1959, *IV* 834–838.

to perform for alms in grotesque symmetry.[9] 'The Chimney Sweeper' is saying to the London citizen: you salve your conscience by handing out a few farthings on May Day, but if you really listened to this bitter cry among the snow you and your icy church would be appalled.

When we turn now to 'London', Blake's 'mightiest brief poem',[10] our minds ringing with Blakean themes, we come upon infinite curses in a little room, a world at war in a grain of London soot. On the illuminated page a child is leading a bent old man along the cobblestones and a little vagabond is warming his hands at a fire in the open street. But it is Blake who speaks. . . .

In his first draft Blake wrote 'dirty street' and 'dirty Thames' as plain statement of fact, reversing the sarcastic 'golden London' and 'silver Thames' of his early parody of Thomson's 'Rule Britannia'. And the harlot's curse sounded in every 'dismal' street. The change to 'charter'd' (with an intermediate 'cheating')[11] mocks Thomson's boast that 'the charter of the land' keeps Britons free, and it suggests agreement with (perhaps was even suggested by) Paine's condemnation of 'charters and corporations' in the Second Part of *The Rights of Man*, where Paine argues that all charters are purely negative in effect and that city charters, by annulling the rights of the majority, cheat the inhabitants and destroy the town's prosperity—even London being 'capable of bearing up against the political evils of a corporation' only from its advantageous situation on the Thames.[12] Paine's work was circulated by shopkeepers chafing under corporation rule and weary, like Blake, of the 'cheating waves of charter'd streams' of monopolized commerce (*N.* 113).

In the notebook fragment just quoted Blake speaks of shrinking 'at the little blasts of fear That the hireling blows into my ear', thus indicating that when he writes of the 'mind-forg'd manacles' in every cry of fear and every ban he is not saying simply that people are voluntarily forging manacles in their own minds. Hireling informers or mercenaries promote the fear; Pitt's proclamations are the bans, linked with an order to dragoons 'to assemble on Hounslow Heath' and

---

[9] I refer to an ancient May Day custom, illustrated by Blake in 1784 in an engraving for the *Wit's Magazine*, after Collings. The picture, *May Day*, is still used in works illustrating social customs. Milkmaids danced with pitcher-laden trays on their heads; the sweeps, with wigs to cover their grimy heads, banged their brushes and scrapers in rhythm; and a fiddler or two supplied a tune. Reproduced in *Johnson's England*, ed. A. S. Turberville, I, 174.

[10] Oliver Elton's phrase, I forgot where.

[11] The 'cheating' variant is in *N.* 113; see E464, 772/K166.

[12] Paine, I, 407; Nancy Bogen (*Notes and Queries*, xv, January 1968) finds Paine also calling 'every chartered town . . . an aristocratic monopoly' in the First Part (1791) as well. On chartered boroughs see Cowper, *The Task*, iv. 671; also John Butler, *Brief Reflections*, 1791, a pamphlet reply to Burke cited in J. T. Boulton, *The Language of Politics in the Age of Wilkes and Burke*, Toronto, 1963, p. 193.

E

'be within one hour's march of the metropolis'.[13] A rejected reading, 'german forged links', points to several manacles forged ostensibly in the mind of Hanoverian George: the Prussian manoeuvres on the heath, the British alliance with Prussia and Austria against France, and the landing of Hessian and Hanoverian mercenaries in England allegedly en route to battlefronts in France.

Blake may have written 'London' before this last development, but before he completed his publication there was a flurry of alarm among freeborn Englishmen at the presence of German hirelings. 'Will you wait till BARRACKS are erected in every village,' exclaimed a London Corresponding Society speaker in January 1794, 'and till subsidized Hessians and Hanoverians are upon us?'[14] In Parliament Lord Stanhope expressed the hope that honest Britons would meet this Prussian invasion 'by OPPOSING FORCE BY FORCE'. And the editor of *Politics for the People*, reporting that one Hessian had stabbed an Englishman in a street quarrel, cried that all were brought 'to cut the throats of Englishmen'. He urged citizens to arm and to fraternize with their fellow countrymen, the British common soldiers.[15]

The latter are Blake's 'hapless Soldiers' whose 'sigh Runs in blood down Palace walls'—and whose frequently exhibited inclination in 1792-1793 to turn from grumbling to mutiny[16] is not taken into account by those who interpret the blood as the soldier's own and who overlook the potentially forceful meaning of 'sigh' in eighteenth century diction.[17] In the structure of the poem the soldier's utterance

---

[13] *Gazette*, Dec. 1, 1792. In the note just cited, Mrs Bogen suggests that Blake's choice, in the Thames poem, of the Ohio as the river to wash Thames stains from a Londoner 'born a slave' and aspiring 'to be free' was influenced by Gilbert Imlay's *Topographical Description*, London, 1792. On the Ohio Imlay found escape from 'musty forms' that 'lead you into labyrinths of doubt and perplexity' and freedom from priestcraft which elsewhere 'seems to have forged fetters for the human mind'.

[14] Address at Globe Tavern, Jan. 20, 1794 (pamphlet).

[15] Eaton, *Politics for the People*, II, no. 7, March 15, 1794.

[16] The Royal Proclamation cited efforts to 'delude the judgment of the lower classes' and 'debauch the soldiery'. Wilberforce feared that 'the soldiers are everywhere tampered with'. Gilbert Elliot in November expressed a common belief that armies and navies would prove 'but brittle weapons' against the spreading French ideas. *Life and Letters of Sir Gilbert Elliot First Earl of Minto*, 3 vols., London, 1874, II, 74. Through the winter and spring there were sporadic attacks of the populace on press gangs and recruiting houses. Mutiny and rumours of mutiny were reported in the *General Evening Post*, Apr. 20, July 20, Aug. 3, 7, 31, Oct. 28, 30, 1793. In Ireland the mutiny of embodied regiments broached into a small civil war. See also Lucyle Werkmeister, *A Newspaper History of England*, 1792–1793, Lincoln, Neb., 1968, items indexed under 'Insurrection, phantom', and 'Ireland'.

[17] S. Foster Damon, *William Blake: His Philosophy and Symbols*, Boston and London, 1924, p. 283, reads it as the battlefield 'death-sigh' which morally 'is a stain upon the State'. Joseph H. Wicksteed, *Blake's Innocence & Experience*, N.Y., 1928, p. 253, has it that the soldier who promotes peace is quelling the

that puts blood on palace walls is parallel to the harlot's curse that blasts and blights. And Blake would have known that curses were often chalked or painted on the royal walls. In October 1792 Lady Malmesbury's Louisa saw 'written upon the Privy Garden-wall, "No coach-tax; d——Pitt! d——n the Duke of Richmond! *no King*" '.[18]

A number of cognate passages in which Blake mentions blood on palace walls indicate that the blood is an apocalyptic omen of mutiny and civil war involving regicide. In *The French Revolution* people and soldiers fraternize, and when their 'murmur' (sigh) reaches the palace, blood runs down the ancient pillars. In *The Four Zoas*, Night I, similar 'wailing' affects the people; 'But most the polish'd Palaces, dark, silent, bow with dread.' 'But most' is a phrase straight from 'London'. And in Night IX the people's sighs and cries of fear mount to 'furious' rage, apocalyptic blood 'pours down incessant', and 'Kings in their palaces lie drown'd' in it, torn 'limb from limb'.[19] In the same passage the marks of weakness and woe of 'London' are spelled out as 'all the marks ... of the slave's scourge & tyrant's crown'. In 'London' Blake is talking about what he hears in the streets, not about the moral stain of the battlefield sigh of expiring soldiers.

In Blake's notebook the lines called 'An Ancient Proverb' recapitulate the 'London' theme in the form of a Bastille Day recipe for freeing Old England from further plagues of tyranny:

> Remove away that blackning church
> Remove away that marriage hearse
> Remove away that —— of blood
> You'll quite remove the ancient curse.

Where he might have written 'palace' he cautiously writes a dash.[20] Yet despite the occasional shrinking of Blake as citizen, Blake as prophet, from *The French Revolution* to *The Song of Los*, from 1791 to 1795, cleaved to the vision of an imminent spring thaw when the happy earth would 'sing in its course' as the fire of Voltaire and Rousseau melted the Alpine or Atlantic snows. In England, neverthe-

---

'tumult and war' of a 'radically unstable' society. But Blake was not one to look upon riot-quelling as a securing of freedom and peace! Alfred Kazin, *The Portable Blake*, p. 15, with a suggestion 'that the Soldier's desperation runs, like his own blood, in accusation down the walls of the ruling Palace', comes closer to the spirit of indignation which Blake reflects.

[18] Elliot, II, 71. Verbally Blake's epithet may be traced back, I suppose, to 'hapless Warren!', Barlow's phrase for the patriot general dying at Bunker Hill (changed to 'glorious Warren' in 1793).

[19] *F.R.* 241-246: K145; *F.Z.* i.396: K275; ix.73-74, 230-255: K359,363.

[20] *N.*107: E466, 773/K176, 184. Blake's dash, an unusual mark for him, replaces an earlier 'man' which replaced a still earlier 'place'. The 'man of blood' would be the King, but Blake wanted the *place*, i.e. the Palace, and so settled for a dash.

less, the stubborn frost persisted and the wintry dark; and England's crisis and Earth's crisis were threatening to become permanent.

From 'Infinite London', Chapter 13 of *Blake: Prophet Against Empire,* Princeton University Press, Princeton, (1954); revised ed. 1969, pp. 272-9. Revised edition, by Princeton University Press and Doubleday Anchor Books. Copyright (c) 1954, 1969 by Princeton University Press. Reprinted by permission of Princeton University Press.

JOHN H. SUTHERLAND (1955)

Blake's *Mental Traveller*

Different critics have offered startlingly different interpretations of Blake's 'Mental Traveller'. The poem tells the fairly simple story of one cycle in an apparently endless series. The characters in it are obviously symbolical, and most of the different readings of the poem have depended on a number of quite different identifications of them. Thus one may read the poem as an account of the path of the mystic (with Foster Damon); as a sun myth combined with an account of the Incarnation, plus a galaxy of other things esoteric (with Ellis and Yeats); as the story of 'an Explorer of mental phaenomena' and the development of a new idea (with W. M. Rossetti); as the presentation of a version of the Orc cycle (with Mona Wilson or with Northrop Frye); or one may throw up one's hands (as Bernard Blackstone did recently) and say that '*The Mental Traveller* is an extremely cryptic poem in quatrains: as to its meaning, one reader's guess seems as good as another's'.[1]

When one considers that the foregoing list by no means exhausts the variety of suggested readings of the poem, it seems quite clear that there would be little point in merely adding one more possible interpretation. What is needed is an approach which can provide more evidence for the postive identification of symbols. If this is too much to hope for—since a poem is not a mathematical formula—one can at least reaffirm one's faith that the poet did mean something quite definite, and pursue that definite meaning as far as possible.

There are two important methods which can be used in an explication of this sort. One of these has been widely and successfully used on Blake's prophetic works, but has not yet worked as well on this poem as on others: it is to search out parallel figures and situations in Blake's other poems, and thus relate the poem in question to the great myth which Blake created. The other method, although commonly used in the reading of the work of other poets, has not been

[1] See S. Foster Damon, *William Blake, His Philosophy and Symbols*, Boston and New York, 1924, pp. 129–32; Edwin John Ellis and William Butler Yeats, *The Works of William Blake*, London, 1893, II, pp. 34–6; Mona Wilson, *The Life of William Blake*, London, 1932, pp. 156–7 (this includes a long quotation from W. M. Rossetti); Northrop Frye, *Fearful Symmetry*, Princeton University Press, 1947, pp. 227–9; Bernard Blackstone, *English Blake*, Cambridge University Press, 1949, p. 131. The present paper uses, as its most helpful starting point, the excellent analysis in Professor Frye's *Fearful Symmetry*.

applied to Blake's poems as systematically as it might be. It is to pay very close, literal attentions to background, siuation, and point of view in the poe, in the hopes that establishing these things will make the nature and significance of the central figures stand out more clearly and certainly. The present paper uses both these methods, but leans more heavily on the second. It is, frankly, an attempt to present a complete reading of the poem, and to solve all the major difficulties connected with it. Such an arrogant effort robably does not even deserve success, but the method of attack may, in any event, help to further clarify the nature of the puzzle.

One key to the structure of the world as Blake saw it—which is also a necessary key to the background and structure of 'The Mental Traveller'—is to be found in the major prophetic book *Milton*. There Blake makes an admirably plain statement about matters which are often thought to be beyond hope of human comprehension:

> The nature of infinity is this: That every thing has its
> Own Vortex, and when once a traveller thro' Eternity
> Has pass'd that Vortex, he perceives it roll backward behind
> His path, into a globe itself infolding like a sun
> Or like a moon, or like a universe of starry majesty,
> While he keeps onward in his wondrous journey on the earth....[2]

Blake's system seems to have had many affinities with Berkeleian idealism: it presupposed that the only reality is psychological reality, and that the materialism of physicists, chemists, and astronomers is error and self-deception. His theory of vortexes is an amusing, and surprisingly neat, way of explaining figuratively the relationship of the temporal sense data perceived by the individual to the raw material of Eternity and infinity The theory is thoroughly explained in Northrop Frye's *Fearful Symmetry*.[3] Briefly, it amounts to this: The fundamental pattern of visual awareness, as Blake thought of it, took the form of a cone opening into the observer's eyes and mind, and coming to its apex at the object perceived. Thus 'evry thing has its Own Vortex'. An individual on a higher lane of awarness would, depending on his state, either realize that sense data only existed within himself (since, as Berkeley pointed out, the existence of objects depends entirely on their apprehension by a conscious mind), or else would see things as much smaller and more manageable than they appear to the fallen senses of those of us who seem to be at the mercy of the material world.

Such an individual, passing from a higher plane of awareness into the fallen world of the senses, would pass (as it were) *through* objects of apprehension like the sun, moon, and stars. Moving on, down to-

---

[2] *Poetry and Prose of William Blake*, ed. Geoffrey Keynes, London, 1948, p. 392. [*Complete Writings*, ed. Keynes, London, 1957, 1966, p. 497.]

[3] p. 350 *et passim*.

ward Earth, he would pass from the objects into the cones, or vortexes, of the objects. When he looked back, he would see the material of Eternity—contracted to fit his fallen sense organs—roll out behind him like marbles. Instead of seeing something infinitely greater, he would see the globes, balls, and flickers that most people agree to see in the sky at night. Instead of realizing that he, as a perceiving mind, comprehended all matter, he would think of the material world as composed of many frightening things much bigger than himself.

Since fundamental reality was human reality, a mental traveller of this sort could, in one sense, travel without ever leaving this earth. And by this earth Blake did not mean the large, ronnd planet of the astronomers: he meant—in terms of each individual—that the part of the world which was bounded by the limits of one man's apprehension was not only his Earth, but also his Universe:

> The Sky is an immortal Tent built by the Sons of Los:
> And every Space that a Man views around his dwelling-place
> Standing on his own roof or in his garden on a mount
> Of twenty-five cubits in height, such space is his Universe:
> And on its verge the Sun rises & sets, the Clouds bow
> To meet the flat Earth & the Sea in such an order'd Space:
> .   .   .   .
> Such are the Spaces called Earth & such its dimension.
> As to that false appearance which appears to the reasoner
> As of a Globe rolling thro' Voidness, it is a delusion of Ulro.[4]

This seems, at first consideration, to be a very primitive world, since it is limited by the boundaries of one man's senses. However, Blake did not think of it as limited, since he set no limits to the glories which might be apprehended by the senses. To think of the world as Blake did was to deny the validity of that which is seen by the materialistic reasoner; and to deny that was to affirm a belief in much more which might be seen, but which was hidden from the self-deluded reasoner. Each man (each in his own world) could be, like Blake, a mental traveller. Each man was, whether or not he desired it, a traveller through eternity:

> Thus is the earth one infinite plane, and not as apparent
> To the weak traveller confin'd beneath the moony shade.
> Thus is the heaven a vortex pass'd already, and the earth
> A vortex not yet pass'd by the traveller thro' Eternity.[5]

One more pont should be mentioned. Between Earth and Eeternity (or Eden) was another place, a sort of half-way spot which Blake colled Beulah. Blake thought of Beulah as a gentle, shadowy place inhabited by women and children, and connected with ideas of birth and growth. Like Earth, it was a merciful release for those who were unable to face

---

[4] Keynes edn., p. 413. [K. p. 516.]
[5] *Ibid.*, p. 392. [K. p. 497.]

the wonders of Eternity; however, the inhabitants of Beulah were
much closer to the vision of Eternity than to the limitations of Earth:

> There is a place where Contrarieties are equally True:
> This place is called Beulah. It is a pleasant lovely Shadow
> Where no dispute can come, Because of those who Sleep.
>
> . . . .
>
> Beulah is evermore Created around Eternity, appearing
> To the Inhabitants of Eden around them on all sides.
> But Beulah to its Inhabitants appears within each district
> As the beloved infant in his mother's bosom round incircled
> With arms of love & pity & sweet compassion. But to
> The Sons of Eden the moony habitations of Beulah
> Are from Great Eternity a mild & pleasant Rest.
>
> . . . .
>
> And the Shadows of Beulah terminate in rocky Albion.[6]

With this much of the stage set, a close examination of 'The Mental
Traveller' can be attempted. Enough has been said to make it pos-
sible to establish background and point of view in the poem. It is
hoped that the precise nature of the background will become clearer
as the discussion progresses.

The first stanza sets the scene where over half the story takes place.
It also establishes the point of view, since it identifies the poet Blake
as the mental traveller who sees and reports all that happens. He says:

> I Travel'd thro' a Land of Men,
> A Land of Men & Women too,
> And heard & saw such dreadful things
> As cold Earth wanderers never knew.[7]

The last line of this stanza makes it clear that the stage is not Earth
as seen by limited human beings. Later on in the poem a descent to
the world of the senses indicates that what went before was on a much
larger scale. To put an arbitrary name to it at the beginning, we might
say that the stage is set somewhere in Eternity—evidence further on
may enable us to be somewhat more specific when we come to it. The
'Men & Women' who inhabit Eternity are risen, giant forms; they
have a great deal more energy and significance than the 'nonpeople'
(as e. e. cummings would call them) that we see around us every day.
Moreover, knowing Blake's other poems, it seems a safe guess to say
that some of these figures must be archetypes, or eternal forms, of
forces which manifest themselves in a different way on this earth.

The final stanza demonstrates that the whole poem is devoted to the
account of a cyclical process. This has led a number of critics to look

---

[6] *Ibid.*, pp. 415–16. [K. p. 518.]

[7] *Ibid.*, pp. 110–13. All subsequent quotations from 'The Mental Traveller'
are taken from these pages. [K. pp. 424-7.]

for parallels between the story of the male Babe and the so-called 'Orc cycle'. The parallels are genuine and instructive, particularly during the early part of the poem; however, the male Babe's experiences are more complex than Orc's simple rise, stagnation, and fall.

When read in the light of this comparison, the early stanzas offer little difficulty. The Orc-like male Babe (probably representing repressed principles of energy and creative power) is nailed to a rock, like Prometheus, while the 'Woman Old' (probably representing Nature) tortures him, and 'lives upon his shrieks & cries'. This diet seems to agree with her, since 'she grows young as he grows old'.

In stanzas six and seven, the Babe, grown up, subdues the woman (now a young virgin), rapes her, and thus makes Nature, or Mother Earth, his '... dwelling place/ And Garden fruitful seventy fold'. This is a symbolic statement of a universal historical truth. It has led to the male Babe being taken to represent a variety of different movements and ideas, since religions, philosophies, and civilizations—as well as individual men—have risen to subdue and cultivate the world that tyrannized them in their infancies. Similar symbolic relationships may be found in the stories of major gods of antiquity.[8] It seems obvious that identifying the male Babe as being akin to the Orc-principle satisfies the general truth of the allegory better than any more specific reading possibly could.

The Babe does not retain his youthful vigour very long. The eighth stanza refers to him as an 'aged Shadow ... / Wand'ring round an Earthly Cot'. This 'Cot', or cottage, is described as being filled with 'gems & gold/ Which he by industry had got'.

The 'aged Shadow', as has been pointed out before, has much in common with the figure which Blake elsewhere calls Urizen.[9] Orc, the youthful, archetypal spirit of revolt, after having achieved his minimum goals, all too naturally hardens into the conservative spirit of order and oppression. As the Jehovah-like Urizen, the spirit hurts and destroys just because he wishes to preserve things without change.

All this takes place in terms of particular scenes and circumstances, as observed by Blake, the mental traveller. The aged Shadow is in Eternity still, but is becoming more and more bound and limited to the physical world. The symbol of this is the 'Earthly Cot', which seems to be either the Earth, or else another planet like the Earth. (Such worlds of the fallen senses are, to a mental traveller, no more than cottages—temporary dwelling places of the soul.)

The 'gems & gold' with which the aged Shadow filled the Earth are explained in stanza nine. They are 'the gems of the Human Soul'— which is to say that they are made up of various manifestations of human suffering. 'The martyr's groan & the lover's sigh' to which

[8] Frye, p. 228.
[9] Cf. *ibid.*, p. 229.

Blake refers in this stanza can be compared with these famous lines from 'The Grey Monk':

> For a Tear is an Intellectual Thing,
> And a Sigh is the Sword of an Angel King,
> And the bitter groan of the Martyr's woe
> Is an Arrow from the Almightie's Bow.[10]

Tyrants (both earthly and archetypal) delight in human suffering. Blake didn't like either tyrants or suffering, but he recognized their inevitable place in the organization of a fallen world.

In 'The Mental Traveller', Blake is intensely, and ironically, aware of the value of suffering to the tyrant: 'They [groans and sighs] are his meat, they are his drink.' Blake is purposely ironic as he records the aged Shadow's generosity with this kind of riches: 'He feeds the Beggar & the Poor.' His door is 'for ever open' to those who are vulnerable to human pain. Moreover, this is a give-and-take arrangement. The groans and sighs seem to be deliberately conceived as ambivalent: they are produced by poor, oppressed mortals for the delectation of the tyrant Shadow, and they are distributed as food (or in lieu of food) to the poor and oppressed by the Shadow.

This is the normal end of the Orc cycle. The next step would be the breakdown of the static and corrupt establishment, a falling back into a period of gestation, and then the rebirth of the young spirit to repeat the process. However, as a mental traveller with creative vision, Blake did not see man as inexorably caught by such a pagan nightmare. Stanza eleven records what can happen if people in the cottage (i.e., on earth) find, to the aged Shadow's grief, some way of exercising their creative powers:

> His [the Shadow's] grief is their eternal joy;
> They make the roofs & walls [heaven and earth] to ring;
> Till from the fire on the hearth
> A little Female Babe does spring.

The Female Babe springs from fire—symbolically the source of energy and inspiration. She is described in stanza twelve as being 'all of solid fire/ And gems & gold'—so awe-inspiring that no one dares to touch her. The aged Shadow (in stanza thirteen called the 'aged Host') fears and hates this splendid product of man's creative powers. He feeds on man's grief; it makes perfect sense that the creative imagination, which can free man from grief, is the source of his grief. In terms of the ideas symbolized, the exact, mechanical, and limiting principles in the universe must have something to limit in order to exist at all. Thus, when applied to man, they exist, literally, because of man's grief. When men find their way through to some source of

[10] Keynes edn., p. 118. [K. p. 430.]

creative energy, they free themselves and bring grief to that power which previously had oppressed them.

In stanza thirteen, the Female Babe is presented as an archetypal spirit closely akin to a muse. She is described as coming 'to the Man she loves' (the artist, and perhaps the mystic and the saint); together, the man and the Female Babe drive out 'the aged Host,/ A Beggar at another's door'. (Here 'the Man she loves' seems to be primarily the human individual, who can, through creative inspiration, free himself from the dead hand of Urizen; however, it may also refer to mankind as a whole, since the fate of the aged Host after he loses his kingdom is described in symbolic terms which can apply at any level. He could be losing control of one man and one man's world; he could also be losing control of the whole planet, as mankind now knows it through its fallen senses.)

Once Urizen has been driven out, he tries, more and more desperately, to find some person or thing to impose himself on. He finally wins a 'Maiden':

> And to allay his freezing Age
> The Poor Man takes her in his arms;
> The Cottage fades before his sight,
> The Garden & its lovely Charms.

The maiden seems to represent materialism and the world of the fallen senses. The aged Shadow, now appropriately called the 'Poor Man', embraces materialism as a last resort, and very naturally falls out of the world of archetypes in Eternity into the limited world which is the lowest common denominator of sensory apprehension. There is nothing said here of vortexes, in the sense Blake used the term when explaining the nature of infinity in *Milton*; however, it is quite clear that the aged Shadow has passed through the vortexes of the material world and now sees things from a point of view similar to that of a person on this earth. In Eternity, Earth was but a cottage, and its inhabitants were all together. To the fallen senses, Earth seems a vast ball, and its inhabitants appear to be separated by great distances:

> The Guests are scatter'd thro' the land,
> For the Eye altering alters all;
> The Senses roll themselves in fear,
> And the flat Earth becomes a Ball;
>
> The stars, sun, Moon, all shrink away,
> A desart vast without a bound,
> And nothing left to eat or drink,
> And a dark desart all around.

Although Blake does not say so directly anywhere in the poem, it seems likely that the maiden the cast-out aged Host turns to is a frustrated female Babe, grown older without finding 'the Man she

loves'. Just as it was natural for the male Babe, Orc, to cease to repre-
sent energy and revolt, so it is natural for a female Babe—once a
muse—to degenerate into a coquette and sensualist. It is noteworthy
that sensuality and the artifices of physical and emotional love have an
entirely different effect on her than they do on the aged Shadow. His
part is to pursue the fleeting pleasure of simple indulgence, and this,
very naturally, makes an infant of him. Her part is to lead him through
'Labyrinths of wayward Love' by means of 'various arts of Love &
Hate'. Just as naturally, this makes an old woman of her.

There is violence and inaccuracy in the giving of abstract equiva-
lents for these figures at any of the stages of their development. How-
ever, if one allows for that, it seems illuminating to consider the direct
proportion here suggested: the female Babe is to the Maiden (who
becomes the weeping Woman Old), as the male Babe is to the bleed-
ing youth (who becomes the aged Host). This is to say: creative
imagination is to sexual love (which ages into the cruelty of 'Mother'
Nature), as creative energy is to physical construction (which ages into
the conservative principle of tyranny and repression).

The principal weakness of this proportion is that it suggests static
balance while Blake is talking about cyclical flux. The relationship of
the two figures in the poem follows the general line of the relationship
in the proportion, but it is dynamic, and constantly shifting, as is
necessary for the continuation of their cyclical existence. Near the end
of the poem, the conservative principle reverts again to infancy as it is
betrayed and teased in the world of the senses. The cycle is completed
when 'he becomes a wayward Babe,/ And she a weeping Woman
Old'. At the same time they return from out the fallen world into
Eternity as 'The Sun & Stars are nearer roll'd'. (Note that most of
these relationships are supported directly by the text of the poem.
The hypothetical connection between the female Babe and the Maiden
only adds detail to the structure.)

The return to Eternity does not involve physical travelling—it is
brought about by an improvement in the sense organs. In *The Mar-
riage of Heaven and Hell* Blake explains the process this way:

> If the doors of perception were cleansed every thing would appear
> to man as it is, infinite.
> For man has closed himself up, till he sees all things thro' narrow
> chinks of his cavern.[11]

In 'The Mental Traveller', the improvement in apprehension seems
to come at least partly because of the improvement in environment.
Paradoxically, although the fall seems to have been partially due to
fear ('The Senses roll themselves in fear,/ And the flat Earth becomes
a Ball'), the planting of the desert is also partly due to fear ('Like the
wild Stag she flees away,/ Her fear plants many a thicket wild.').

[11] *Ibid.*, p. 187. [K. p. 154.]

Those thickets which are not due to fear are the result of a kind of love which is very closely related to fear: '... the wide desart planted o'er/ With Labyrinths of wayward Love,/ Where roam the Lion, Wolf & Boar.' Thus, that which helped cause the fall from Eternity is an indirect cause of the temporary regaining of Eternity.

These thickets of passion are very like those described in greater detail in some of the *Songs of Experience* ('A Poison Tree', 'The Garden of Love', 'My Pretty Rose-Tree'). They are far from being happy products, but they are—like the jungle—symbols of simple fertility. As such, they are a necessary background to the development of love, and to the growth of cities and civilization. Love and civilization represented creative achievement to Blake; he thought of them as important stages on the road to seeing things (at least partially) in their eternal forms. Thus, at the very time that the thickets of love have made a Babe of the aged Host, and a Woman Old of the Maiden, they have made an environment in which 'many a Lover wanders', and which helps bring about the return to Eternity.

Immediately after the return, Blake describes the background this way:

> The trees bring forth sweet Extacy
> To all who in the desert roam;
> Till many a City there is Built,
> And many a pleasant Shepherd's home.

When taken in conjunction with details of the thickets of love, this stanza seems to suggest more precisely the part of Eternity involved than do the earlier sections of the poem. Beulah, the land of generation, has much in common with this place. It is in Eternity, but on the edges of Eternity, from which it is easy to fall into the material world. It is a seed place, whose inhabitants are preoccupied with sex, love, and growth. Thus one of the things the poem seems to be saying is that the Platonic ladder of love is inadequate: that the cycle here described touches, as its high point, the three-fold vision of Beulah, and then swings back inevitably into the thraldom of the material world.

Men may be subject to the terms of this cycle, or they may win free of them. The poem has nothing to do with the question of human reincarnation, and Blake is only indirectly concerned with ways in which man may find Eternity. Although stanza thirteen suggests, as we have seen, that a man may unite with a female Babe to drive out the aged Shadow, the poem is really about the dynamic relationships of eternal principles, and hardly about men at all.

At the end of the poem, these principles seem to be doomed to an everlasting repetition of the cycle we have traced. In finding its way back to the edges of Eternity, the male principle is inexorably reduced to hopeless infancy, and thus becomes, again, the male Babe, whose 'frowning form' is so terrible (because of the potentialities it represents) that all flee from it. The only one who dares touch it is the Maiden, who has again become 'a Woman Old'. She nails it to a rock again, as another cycle commences.

'Blake's "Mental Traveller" ', *Journal of English Literary History*, (*ELH*), vol. XXII, 1955, pp. 136–47. (c) The Johns Hopkins Press.

ROBERT F. GLECKNER (1956)

Irony in Blake's *Holy Thursday*

The general ironic tone of Blake's account of charity children in 'Holy Thursday' (*Songs of Innocence*) has been frequently noted: though the children seem happy they were often flogged, poorly fed, and annually forced to march through the streets to St Paul's to give thanks for the 'kindnesses' they had received during the year, and to celebrate the anniversary of the founding of the schools. Blake's irony, however, is even more profound and pervasive than has been noticed: it takes into account not only the schools themselves but the entire concept of professional charity symbolized in the poem by the beadles who rule over the procession, by the regimentation of the children and the colourful uniforms they wear, and by the 'wise guardians of the poor'.

Though we do not know whether Blake himself actually saw one of these processions before he wrote the poem,[1] clearly he was aware of the public's sentimental approval of them: it was indeed a 'spectacle pleasing both to God and man', as Addison wrote in *The Guardian*, No. 105.[2] Bernard Mandeville was somewhat differently impressed as his 'Essay on Charity, and Charity Schools' of 1723 reveals. In one passage of this notorious and widely read essay, after showing how public opinion of 'slovenly sorry Fellows' changes once they don bright red uniforms and grenadier's caps, Mandeville applies this idea to the uniformed charity children:

There is something Analogous to this in the Sight of Charity Children; there is a natural Beauty in Uniformity which most People delight in. It is diverting to the Eye to see children well match'd, either Boys or Girls, march two and two in good order; and to have them all whole and tight in the same Clothes and Trimming must add to the comeliness of the sight; and what makes it still more generally entertaining is the imaginary share which even Servants and the meanest in the Parish have in it, to whom it costs nothing; Our Parish Church, Our Charity Children. In all this there is a Shadow of Property that tickles every body that

[1] Though Blake was in London during perhaps three of these anniversary celebrations the chance of his having seen one before the writing of 'Holy Thursday' is, at best, slight. The services were not held in St Paul's until 1782 and Blake's poem was written about 1784.

[2] For other contemporary accounts in the same vein see D. V. Erdman, *Blake: Prophet Against Empire*, Princeton, 1954, p. 111, and M. G. Jones, *The Charity School Movement*, Cambridge, 1938, pp. 59–61.

has a Right to make use of the Words, but more especially those who actually contribute and had a great Hand in advancing the pious Work (F. B. Kaye, ed., *The Fable of the Bees: or, Private Vices, Publick Benefits*, Oxford, 1924, 1, 281-2).

Though the idea, language, tone, and an occasional phrase of this passage are similar to Blake's poem, it is not my intention to claim it as a source, but rather to suggest that Blake's *method* of attack upon 'charity' is similar to Mandeville's: both men reveal, ironically, that the schools were based not on kindness, altruism, and Christian charity, but upon the self-love and what Mandeville called the 'private vices' of their sponsors.

Mandeville's reference to the coloured uniform is especially interesting since Blake, too, clothes his children in bright colours ('red and blue and green'), despite the fact that charity school uniforms were usually drab 'to drive home the lessons of poverty, humility, and submission'.[3] It is possible, of course, that Blake intended the coloured suits and dresses to be the children's Sunday finery, put on to brighten the occasion; and it is true that there were several charity schools known by the colour of their uniforms.[4] But in this light Mandeville's attack is all the more valid, and Blake's regimented procession becomes pure sham—sham pleasantness, sham 'cleanliness', sham relief from poverty, sham charity.[5]

In the last stanza of 'Holy Thursday' Blake's irony reaches its peak, partly because he employs the title officially given to the beneficent patrons of charity schools. In this stanza the children demonstrate their essential innocence, despite the attempts to make them conform to a hypocritical regimen, by spontaneously, 'like a mighty wind', raising their voices to heaven in song. Instantly the wooden galleries in which they sit[6] seem transformed into the 'seats of Heaven'. Beneath

[3] Jones, p. 75.

[4] For example, the Grey Coat Hospital in Westminster and the Green Coat Hospital in Cork.

[5] Similarly Mandeville's view that the virtues of society are a direct result of the vices of individuals anticipates Blake's view in 'The Human Abstract', in which the apparent virtues of worldly pity and mercy are seen to be the result of rationalizing the misery of man. For example, in his essay on charity Mandeville writes 'that in a free Nation where slaves are not allow'd of, the surest Wealth consists in a Multitude of laborious Poor; for besides that they are the never-failing Nursery of Fleets and Armies, without them there could be no Enjoyment, and no Product of any Country could be valuable. To make the Society happy and People easy under the meanest Circumstances, it is requisite that great Numbers of them should be Ignorant as well as Poor' (Kaye, ed., 1, 287–8). And where Blake writes in 'The Human Abstract' that 'mutual fear brings peace, / Till the selfish loves increase', Mandeville writes in Remark (R.) to the *Fable*: 'The only useful Passion then that Man is possess'd of toward the Peace and Quiet of a Society, is his Fear, and the more you work upon it the more orderly and governable he'll be . . .' (Kaye, 1, 206).

[6] "'To accommodate the huge gatherings, estimated at 12,000 persons, wooden galleries were erected at considerable expense to hold 'the little Eleemosynaries'" (Jones, p. 60.)

the children, unable to 'rise' in the same way, 'sit the aged men, wise guardians of the poor', the poor who need, not guarding, but the love which is absent from such professional pity. The title, 'guardians of the poor', was incorporated frequently into the poor laws of the day and has indeed survived in literary usage down to Shaw's *Major Barbara* ('Board of Guardians'). In 1735, for example, a resolution was made in the House of Commons to better the relief and employment of the poor, and in the same year, and again in 1751, one of the committee members who introduced the resolution published a pamphlet which includes a transcription of it. Its 'professional' tone, its 'incorporation' of charity, and its official title for charity administrators all apply to Blake's poem. The following is from the preamble to the resolution:

Whereas several Hospitals and Infirmaries have of late been established and maintained by voluntary Charities, to the great Comfort of the Poor: And whereas such Charities would probably become more general, were Men of great Station, Fortune, and Credit, appointed to receive the Contributions of well-disposed Persons, and to see the same duly applied, by which many of the Poor might be better taken care of, and the Rates for their Maintenance in Time be lessened; be it therefore enacted, That in every County within that Part of *Great Britain* called *England,* and Dominion of *Wales,* every Peer and Lord of Parliament residing within the County, the Lord Lieutenant of the County for the time being residing within the County, the *Custos Rotulorum* for the time being likewise residing in the County, the High Sheriff for the time being, the Knight or Knights of the Shire for the time being, every Bishop, Dean, and Archdeacon for the time being, having Jurisdiction in the County, or any Part thereof, and every Person residing in the County, possessed of Land lying therein, either Freehold or Copyhold, for his own Life, or some greater Estate, of the yearly Value of Three hundred Pounds, registering his Name at some General Quarter Session of the Peace for the said County, shall be a Corporation by the Name of *The Guardians of the Poor* of the said County: ... ([John Hay], *Remarks on the Laws relating to the Poor; with Proposals for their better Relief and Employment,* London, 1751, pp. 71-2).

The final irony of the poem, then, lies in the relationship between this anniversary celebration of professional charity-mongers and Holy Thursday itself, Ascension Day. While the beadles and the wise guardians of the poor raise the children above the poverty of the streets by marching them into the specially-built galleries of St Paul's, the children on their own ('with radiance all their own') ascend through their song far above the physical confines of the 'high dome of Paul's'. Momentarily, at least, they, like Christ, escape the grave of this world, of Blake's 'London'.

Modern Language Notes, vol. LXXI, 1956, pp. 412–15. (c) The Johns Hopkins Press.

Blake's Art: *Images of Wonder*

With a work of art, the essential thing is to experience it. To experience is not the same thing as to understand. It is one thing to enter into the imaginative world of one of Blake's pictures, his poems, or his myths and to feel the images with their strange and unaccountable vistas awakening within. But it is quite another thing to give a satisfactory account of this experience in terms of the understanding. There is much that may be experienced in one of the simplest of Blake's ineffable poems, or pictures, that overflows any attempt to interpret it. For there is always something implied in the work of art which is beyond thought; something lit up for a moment by the imagination, which is beyond words. If we allow ourselves to enter fully into the experience of a work of art, letting go our rational understanding for the moment, we can become immediately aware of this ineffable quality with its expanding life. This is what Blake invites us to do: *If the Spectator could Enter into these Images in his Imagination ... or could make a Friend and Companion of one of these Images of wonder ... then would he arise from his Grave ... then he would be happy.*[1]

But to experience is not the same thing as to understand. Understanding implies a mental formulation, an interpretation according to conceptual knowledge, and it is just in this that it is important to proceed slowly, and with great reservation. It is all too easy to translate art, which contains the unknown hidden in the incipient hint or implication, into familiar patterns of thoughts, or terms of cognition. But in so doing we lose much of what is important in the work of art. To reduce the unknown forthwith into terms of the known is the temptation which must always be resisted in relation to a work of art. It is as unintelligent as to deny that art has any real and immanent meaning which challenges elucidation. With Blake's art, which is concerned with an unusually subtle calibre of experience, it is especially important to enter fully into its imaginative flight. Only later must come the assimilative processes of understanding. But to experience, in this sense, means to be deeply stirred; and this (although it is the fundamental purpose of art) is what many people instinctively avoid.

As a man William Blake was a seer and devotee intent on studying

---

[1] Notes on *A Vision of the Last Judgment*; Keynes, 1925, vol III, pp. 153–4. [K. p. 611.]

life in all its fullness and mystery, and in his art he laboured to express this without translating the unknown into terms of the known. His art expresses the living experience in terms of images and symbols. By this means the potential of meaning is retained in dynamic terms of life and energy. His myths and symbolic figures and personages are intent with implicit meaning, which is not reduced to the familiar word, or concept, or formula; he avoided the labels of conventional knowledge and left his images and symbols undetermined, but still in contact with the flux of life. So Blake's art can open our eyes, and shock us into relationship with the living experience. Out of this experience, when gradually and intelligently assimilated, can grow understanding. But it will be a different sort of understanding, not that of conventional, second-hand knowledge, or of the accepted textbooks. It will be understanding which has gone beyond itself, knows its limitations, and knows that it is but a pale reflection of the reality which transcends it. . . .

From 'On the Understanding of Blake's Art', in *Symbol and Image in William Blake*, O.U.P., Oxford, 1957, pp. 94–5.

ANTHONY F. BLUNT (1959)

Vision and Execution in Blake's Painting

Blake's theories of art and of poetry were based on a whole-hearted and unqualified belief in the power of imagination and the reality of inspiration: 'One power alone makes a poet: Imagination, the Divine Vision.'[1] His own account of his methods of work is perfectly clear but in some ways misleading. He believed himself to be in immediate contact with 'spirits' who revealed to him his visions and inspired his poems: 'I am under the direction of Messengers from Heaven, Daily and Nightly,'[2] he writes, and sometimes he describes their visitations in terms so immediate as to be disturbing: 'The Prophets Isaiah and Ezekiel dined with me, and I asked them....'[3] In the case of his written works he believed his inspiration to be of the most direct kind. Of his long epic *Milton* he writes to his friend Butts: 'I have written this Poem from immediate Dictation, twelve or sometimes twenty or thirty lines at a time, without Premeditation & even against my Will'; and in another letter he says of the same poem: 'I may praise it, since I dare not pretend to be any other than the Secretary; the Authors are in Eternity.'[4] On the other hand, however much he was basically indebted in his poetry to dictation from an external source, he was not a slave to it and like all poets he altered and improved his first drafts. This is proved by manuscripts like the Rossetti Notebook, in which different versions of a poem occur, each of them with deletions and alterations.

It is also clear from one statement by Blake that he used the word *dictation* in a rather special sense. In the *Address* at the beginning of *Jerusalem* he writes: 'When this Verse was first dictated to me, I consider'd a Monotonous Cadence, like that used by Milton & Shakespeare & all writers of English Blank Verse, derived from the modern bondage of Rhyming, to be a necessary and indispensable part of Verse. But I soon found that in the mouth of a true Orator such monotony was not only awkward, but as much a bondage as rhyme itself. I therefore have produced a variety in every line, both of cadences & number of syllables.'[5] That is to say, the actual form of the composition was

[1] *Poetry and Prose*, ed. Keynes, 1927, p. 1024. [2] *Ibid.*, p. 1061.
[3] *Ibid.*, p. 195. [4] *Ibid.*, pp. 1073, 1076.
[5] *Ibid.*, p. 551.

not dictated to the poet who was at liberty to choose his own metre; and we are forced to the conclusion that in this case it was more the ideas than the actual words which came to him from the spirits. It is, however, also probable that Blake possessed to an unusually high degree the faculty not uncommon in a poet of finding whole lines or groups of lines coming into his mind complete without any conscious effort on his part.

His ideas on art are closely similar. His purpose in life, he said, was to 'See Visions, Dream Dreams & prophecy & speak Parables.'[6] For him painting has nothing to do with the imitation of the material world, but is an imaginative art of the same kind as poetry: 'Shall Painting be confined to the sordid drudgery of fac-simile representations of merely mortal and perishing substances, and not be as poetry and music are, elevated into its own proper sphere of invention and visionary conception? No, it shall not be so! Painting, as well as poetry and music, exists and exults in immortal thoughts.'[7]

From certain evidence, particularly from the account left by Cunningham of his making the *Visionary Heads*, one would be led to suppose that Blake suffered from actual delusions. Cunningham tells how Blake used to sit with Varley and Linnell, who would ask him to draw some historical character. A typical passage is the account of his drawing the portraits of William Wallace and Edward I:

He was requested to draw the likeness of William Wallace—the eye of Blake sparkled, for he admired heroes. 'William Wallace!' he exclaimed, 'I see him now, there, there how noble he looks—reach me my things!' Having drawn for some time, with the same care of hand and steadiness of eye, as if a living sitter had been before him, Blake stopped suddenly and said, 'I cannot finish him—Edward the First has stept in between him and me.' 'That's lucky,' said a friend, 'for I want the portrait of Edward too.' Blake took another sheet of paper, and sketched the features of Plantagenet; upon which his Majesty politely vanished, and the artist finished the head of Wallace.[8]

There is some reason to think that in this case Blake deliberately played up to the expectations of Varley and Linnell and may have talked of these appearances as being more like real physical visions than they actually were, but on other occasions he makes his meaning plainer. The passage of which the beginning has been quoted above is significant:

[6] *Ibid.*, p. 1073.
[7] *Ibid.*, p. 794. Cf. also p. 816: 'No Man of Sense ever supposes that copying from Nature is the Art of Painting; if Art is no more than this, it is no better than any other Manual Labour; anybody may do it and the fool often will do it best as it is a work of no Mind,' and p. 819: 'I obstinately adhere to the true Style of Art ... the Art of Invention, not of Imitation. Imagination is My World; this World of Dross is beneath my Notice.'
[8] Cunningham's account is quoted in full by Mona Wilson, *The Life of William lake*, pp. 256 ff.

The Prophets Isaiah and Ezekiel dined with me, and I asked them how they dared so roundly to assert that God spoke to them; and whether they did not think at the time that they would be misunderstood, and so be the cause of imposition.

Isaiah answer'd: 'I saw no God, nor heard any, in a finite organical perception; but my senses discover'd the infinite in every thing, and as I was then perswaded, and remain confirm'd, that the voice of honest indignation is the voice of God, I cared not for consequences, but wrote.'[9]

Gilchrist records an amusing story which brings out the same point in more fanciful form:

At one of Mr Ader's parties . . . Blake was talking to a little group gathered round him, within hearing of a lady whose children had just come home from boarding school for the holidays. 'The other evening,' said Blake, in his usual quiet way, 'taking a walk, I came to a meadow and, at the farthest corner of it, I saw a fold of lambs. Coming nearer, the ground blushed with flowers; and the wattled cote and its woolly tenants were of an exquisite pastoral beauty. But I looked again, and it proved to be no living flock, but beautiful sculpture.' The lady, thinking this a capital holiday show for her children, eagerly interposed: 'I beg pardon, Mr Blake, but *may* I ask *where* you saw this?' 'Here, madam,' answered Blake, touching his forehead.[10]

Blake, therefore, understood the exact nature of his visions, and although he spoke of them as if they were real, he was aware that they were different from the process of seeing the material world. They were real—in fact for him they were more real than the world around him—but they were real in a special sense. His view is summed up in a passage from the *Descriptive Catalogue*:

I assert for My Self that I do not behold the outward Creation & that to me it is hindrance & not Action; it is as the dirt upon my feet, No part of Me. 'What,' it will be Question'd, 'When the Sun rises, do you not see a round disk of fire somewhat like a Guinea?' O no, no, I see an Innumerable company of the Heavenly host crying, 'Holy, Holy, Holy is the Lord God Almighty.'[11]

The artist, that is to say, does not study the material world for its own sake but regards it as a series of symbols behind which lies truth; and this truth can be apprehended provided the artist hrs the key with which to penetrate the mysery. The key is, of course, provided by he imagination. This faculty enables the artist, as Blake says, to see *through* not *with* the eye[12] and so to penetrate beyond the finite to the infinite and to reach direct communion with the divine: 'He who sees the infinite in all things sees God; he who sees the ratio[13] only

[9] *Works*, p. 195.   [10] *Life of Blake*, ed. Todd, 1942, p. 317.   [11] *Ibid.*, p. 844.

[12] *Ibid.*, p. 844. As Senilcourt has pointed out (*William Blake*, p. 73) this idea is very close to one expressed by Plato in the *Theaetetu's*

[13] i.e., that which can be perceived by reason.

sees himself only.'[14] It is this perception of the infinite that distingu-
ishes Blake's vision from allegory or fable: 'Vision or Imagination is
a Representation of what Eternally Exists, Really and Unchangeably.
Fable or Allegory is Form'd by the daughters of Memory. Imagination
is surrounded by the daughters of Inspiration.'[15] And Blake goes on
to explain that allegory and fable are the mode of expression of the
Greeks but that vision is the characteristic of the prophets of the Old
Testament who were inspired by the Poetic or Prophetic genius, the
source of all truth.[16]

The painter must, therefore, not concern himself with visible ap-
pearances but with the eternal truth lying behind them. Holding this
view, Blake was naturally strongly opposed to Reynolds' views about
nature. Reynolds, whose ideas were basically Aristotelian, believed
that the artist could attain to ideal beauty by generalizing from natural
forms. To this Blake has two objections to make. First, you can never
attain anything worth while if you start from nature; you must first
'travel to Heaven'[17] for the vision and then seek in nature the forms
with which to express it. Second, 'To Generalize is to be an Idiot,'[18]
because visions are always particular.

What Blake meant by this idea can be partly deduced from scattered
remarks in his comments on Reynolds' *Discourses* and others in his
Descriptive Catalogue, sometimes referring directly to painting,
sometimes to poetry, but applicable equally to both. Art is not con-
cerned with ideal beauty nor yet with moral qualiies: 'The Whole
Bible is fill'd with Imagination and Visions from End to End and not
with Moral Virtues; that is the baseness of Plato and the Greeks.'[19]
Art is concerned with the eternal characterisics of individuals. In
speaking of Chaucer's *Canerbury Pilgrims* Blake writes: 'Chaucer
makes every one of his characters perfect in his kind; every one is . . .
the image of a class, and not of an imperfect individual. . . . Visions of
these eternal principles or characters of human life appear to poets,
in all ages,'[20] and these eternal principals are the substance of Blake's
visions and the object of art.

[14] *Works,* p. 829.   [15] *Ibid.*, pp. 828 f.
[16] He does, however, allow that a part of real vision is to be found in the works
of ancient Greek and Latin poets, but only as a faint echo of the true inspiration
of the Hebrew prophets (*ibid.*, p. 831). In one context, moreover, he defines the
'Most Sublime Poetry' as 'Allegory addressed to the Intellectual powers, while
it is altogether hidden from the Corporeal Understanding' (*ibid.*, p. 1076), but
this is as part of the defence of the obscurity of his verse and is not meant in
contrast to vision.
[17] *Ibid.*, p. 987. Cf. also p. 989: 'All Forms are Perfect in the Poet's Mind, but
these are not abstracted nor compounded from Nature, but are from Imagina-
tion.'
[18] *Ibid.*, p. 977.
[19] *Ibid.*, p. 1022. The manuscript is difficult to decipher, and it may be correct
to read *business* rather than *baseness.*
[20] *Ibid.*, pp. 787 f.

But, Blake goes on, these characteristics are precise and not general and must be precisely defined. In his description of the painting of the *Last Judgment* he writes: 'General Knowledge is Remote Knowledge; it is in Particulars that Wisdom consists & Happiness too. Both in Art & in Life, General Masses are as Much Art as a Pasteboard Man is Human. Every Man has Eyes, Nose & Mouth; this Every Idiot knows, but he who enters into & discriminates most minutely the Manners & Intentions, the Characters in all their branches, is the alone Wise or Sensible Man, & on this discrimination All Art is founded.'[21]

Each being, therefore, has its own identity or imaginative form, and this form is unchanging in eternity, though subject to apparent change in the material world. 'Harmony and Proportion are Qualities & not Things. The Harmony & Proportion of a Horse are not the same with those of a Bull. Every Thing has its own Harmony & Proportion, Two Inferior Qualities in it. For its Reality is its Imaginative Form.'[22] 'In Eternity one Thing never Changes into another Thing. Each Identity is Eternal ... but Eternal Identity is one thing & Corporeal Vegetation is another thing. Changing Water into Wine by Jesus & into Blood by Moses relates to Vegetable Nature also.'[23]

Naturally this belief in the fundamental importance of specific characteristics brings Blake into sharp conflict with Reynolds, who held the view that too marked character was incompatible with ideal beauty. 'Leanness or Fatness is not Deformity,' says Blake, 'but Reynolds thought Character Itself Extravagance & Deformity. Age & Youth are not Classes, but Properties of Each Class; so are Leanness & Fatness.'[24] When Reynolds writes: 'Peculiar marks, I hold to be, generally, if not always defects,' Blake comments: 'Peculiar Marks are the Only Merit'; and when on the next page Reynolds repeats the same idea in different words: 'Peculiarities in the works of art, are like those in the human figure: ... they are always so many blemishes', Blake bursts out: 'Infernal Falsehood!'[25] In the previous *Discourse* Reynolds had already incurred Blake's wrath by writing: 'If you mean to preserve the most perfect beauty in its most perfect state, you cannot express the passions', to which Blake retaliates: 'What Nonsense! Passion & Expression is Beauty Itself.'[26]

It is, therefore, the primary business of the artist to express with the greatest clarity the characteristics of the persons whom he depicts, and this clarity demands the highest possible degree of precision and definition. This is the basis for Blake's constantly repeated demand for sharpness of outline and minuteness of detail. 'Where there are no

---

[21] *Ibid.*, pp. 836 f. In another passage from the same account (pp. 829 f) Blake expresses the same idea in almost Platonic terms.

[22] *Ibid.*, p. 1022.   [23] *Vegetable* is Blake's normal word for *material*.

[24] *Ibid.*, p. 990.   [25] *Ibid.*, p. 1005.   [26] *Ibid.*, p. 997.

lineaments there can be no character.'[27] 'Neither character nor expression can exist without firm and determinate outline ... the more distinct, sharp, and wiry the bounding line, the more perfect the work of art, and the less keen and sharp, the greater is the evidence of weak imitation, plagiarism, and bungling.... How do we distinguish the oak from the beech, the horse from the ox, but by the bounding outline? ... Leave out this line, and you leave out life itself.'[28]

Blake maintained, moreover, that his visions were not, as might be supposed, vague and undefined but sharp and minutely clear. 'A Spirit and a Vision are not, as the modern philosophy supposes, a cloudy vapour, or a nothing: they are organized and minutely articulated beyond all that the mortal and perishing nature can produce. He who does not imagine in stronger and better lineaments, and in stronger and better light than his perishing and mortal eyes can see, does not imagine at all. The painter of this work[29] asserts that all his imaginations appear to him infinitely more perfect and more minutely organized than anything seen by his mortal eye.'[30] 'Nature has no Outline, but Imagination has.'[31] And since visions are of this kind, they can only be properly recorded in a work of art by 'minutely Appropriate Execution'.[32]

Blake demands the same clarity in colour as in outline, and it is this view that leads to his loathing, repeated on almost every page of his writings on painting, for all the schools based on colour in the modern sense, all the Venetians, Rubens, and Rembrandt. Blake's attacks on these schools are too well-known to be repeated in detail;[33] one example will give the flavour of them:

> You must agree that Rubens was a Fool,
> And yet you make him master of your School
> And give more money for his slobberings
> Than you will give for Rafael's finest Things.
> I understood Christ was a Carpenter
> And not a Brewer's Servant, my good Sir.[34]

The basis of his attack on the colourists is that the broken colour, the

---

[27] *Ibid.*, pp. 792 f.   [28] *Ibid.*, pp. 805 f.

[29] The painting of *The Bard* from Gray.   [30] *Works*, p. 795.   [31] *Ibid.*, p. 769.

[32] *Ibid.*, p. 814. Blake's whole emphasis on the importance of outline is in essence a variation on Michelangelo's concept of *disegno*, which he would have known through Vasari.

[33] Typical examples are to be found in the *Descriptive Catalogue* (in *Works*, pp. 778 f., 802 f., 818), the epigrams (*ibid.*, pp. 851 ff.) and throughout the comments on Reynolds.

[34] *Works*, p. 851. The word *slobbering* seems to have been a common term of contempt. It is used, for instance, by John Thelwall to Coleridge and explained as meaning 'the drivelling of decayed intellect'. See *Letters of Coleridge*, London and Boston, 1895, I, 200, n. 2.

sfumato and the *chiaroscuro* of the Venetians, destroys the outline and therefore takes away what is most essential in the art of painting.[35]

For Blake, therefore, the creation of a work of art starts with a sharply defined vision which has to be recorded in the clearest possible manner. Though the vision is the starting point in this process, the execution is also essential, and it would give quite a false impression of Blake's aims and methods to over-emphasize the visionary aspect of his art and to slur over the practical.

In some cases it is possible to follow the process by which Blake arrived at his final rendering. In the case of the *Creation of Eve,* for instance, the first sketch is a mere notation in a few rapidly drawn lines of the poses of the three figures, with no indication of anatomical detail and no hint of a setting. In a second version, in water-colour, greater precision is given to the drawing and the poses are slightly altered; the arm of God the Father is raised a little, giving greater solemnity to the gesture of creation; the pose of Adam indicates more positively the complete relaxation of sleep and the leaf-like form on which he lies is more clearly defined; the crescent moon is moved, so that it is exactly above the figure of Eve and the hand of God. In the final composition the whole design is elaborated in detail: the 'leaf' on which Adam lies is edged with flame-like tongues and the trees in the background are articulated with a minute, jewelled *cloisonné* effect.

Another clear example is to be seen in the design of *Satan Smiting Job,* which Blake repeated several times during the later years of his life. His final statement of the composition is the tempera painting in the Tate Gallery, executed only a short time after the engraved version for the *Illustrations of the Book of Job* but fundamentally different from it.[36] In the tempera Blake has given Satan a huge pair of bat's wings, which provide a new formal theme for the design as a whole. The cusped shape of the wings is echoed in inverted form by the cloud behind Satan, and again in the outer radiance of the setting sun.

---

[35] In his attacks on the colourists Blake follows Barry very closely, even to the use of certain characteristic terms, such as the adjective *slobbering* applied to Rubens.

[36] Before the engravings Blake made two sets of water-colours, one for Butts, one for Linnell (see Binyon and Keynes, *Illustrations of the Book of Job*). The third set, the so-called New Zealand set of drawings, was certainly made after the engravings and combines elements from the latter and from the Linnell water-colours. The fact that it contains nothing which is not to be found in one or other of these sources is a strong argument for thinking that the set was not executed by Blake, and this view is confirmed by the technique, which, though exquisite, is more that of Blake's followers, such as Samuel Palmer or Calvert. I am inclined to believe that these water-colours are copies by one or other of these artists, who would have been in a position to know both the engravings and the Linnell water-colours.

The result is a sharpness and brilliance of design entirely lacking in the engraved version.

In evolving his designs, therefore, Blake makes use of the ordinary methods employed by more conventional artists, and in yet another way his manner of work was unexpectedly close to the academic practice of his own time. It may seem paradoxical, but it is true to say that Blake, who was by far the most original English artist of his time, borrowed more extensively and more systematically from the works of other artists than did any of his contemporaries. It was, of course, a doctrine accepted since the sixteenth century that an artist should train himself by studying the works of the great masters and should incorporate in his painting motives borrowed from them, an idea which had been given its fullest expression in the *Discourses* of Sir Joshua Reynolds. Blake's method of borrowing is, however, different. Reynolds, following the academic doctrine of French and Italian art in the seventeenth century, not only wished the artist to borrow and adapt poses or themes from the strictly limited canon of accepted masters, but encouraged him to emulate the style of these masters. With Blake, however, we find that, although his chief admiration was, as we have seen, for Raphael, Michelangelo, and the artists of the Middle Ages, he was prepared to borrow ideas from a very much wider range of works, some of them relatively trivial in quality. Secondly, except in the case of the masters whom he revered, he makes no attempt to imitate the style of those from whom he pilfers ideas. When he borrows a pose from some other artist, he so completely transforms the figure that it seems to be wholly Blakean and shows at first sight no trace of its alien origin. Indeed it seems probable that Blake was often unaware that he was borrowing, and, when he was once challenged on an individual case, he denied that he had ever seen the original which he was accused of imitating. The evidence to show that he did borrow extensively is, however, overwhelming, and one is forced to conclude that Blake's visual memory was so remarkable that, if he had once seen an image, it was retained in the great storehouse of his imagination, together with thousands of other images derived from nature, or other works of art, or the invention of his own fantasy. In fact the same process seems to have taken place in his paintings as in his thought, for ideas from a hundred philosophers, theologians, and poets were absorbed into his mind and emerged, blended and altered, in the rich if tortuous web of the Prophetic Books.

The range of sources from which Blake derived visual themes is surprisingly wide, particularly for an artist of his time. He draws not only on the obvious models, such as Greek and Roman sculpture or engravings after the great masters of the sixteenth century, and on mediaeval sculpture, of which, as we have seen, he was an enthusiastic admirer, but also, more surprisingly, on works of oriental art which were beginning to be known in his day.[37]...

[37] For a more detailed treatment of Blake's sources, see C. H. Collins Baker, *Huntingdon Library Quarterly*, IV, 1941, p. 359, and the present writer's article in the *Journal of the Warburg and Courtauld Institutes*, VI, 1943, pp. 190–212.

From 'Vision and Execution in Blake's Painting', in *The Art of William Blake*, Columbia University Press, New York, 1959, pp. 22–33.

R. D. LAING (1960)

The Divided Self

... In many schizophrenics, the self-body split remains the basic one. However, when the 'centre' fails to hold, neither self-experience nor body experience can retain identity, integrity, cohesiveness, or vitality, and the individual becomes precipitated into a condition the end result of which ... could best be described as a state of 'chaotic nonentity'.
.. The best description of any such condition I have been able to find in literature is in the Prophetic Books of William Blake. In the Greek descriptions of Hell, in Dante, the shades or ghosts, although estranged from life, still retain their inner cohesiveness. In Blake, this is not so. The figures of his Books undergo division in themselves. These books require prolonged study, not to elucidate Blake's psychopathology, but in order to learn from him what, somehow, he knew about in a most intimate fashion, while remaining sane. ...

The Divided Self, Tavistock Publications Ltd, London, 1960, Penguin edition 1965, p. 162.

Albion and Jerusalem

... Blake's 'Patriarch of the Atlantic' whom he calls Albion grows into his final stature from those heroes, titans or gods seen by the writers of cosmogonies, when they looked back towards the horizon of time when heaven and earth were one. Since Greek mythology produced from the union of heaven and earth Saturn or Cronus, the ruler of the golden age, it is not surprising that Holinshed, the Elizabethan chronicler, placed Albion in this first period of the world. In Milton's version of the fable, he is called 'Son of Neptune' and is said to have made an incursion into Gaul in aid of his brother against Hercules.[1] Holinshed, however, furnishes a story which is more in line with Blake's initial use of the myth.

This Albion (that thus changed the name of this Ile) and his company, are called giants, which signifieth none other than a tall kind of men, of that vncorrupted stature and highnesse naturallie incident to the first age (which Berosus also seemeth to allow, where he writeth, that Noah was one of the giants) and were not so called only of their monstrous greatnesse, as the common people thinke (although indeed they exceeded the vsuall stature of men in these daies) but also for that they tooke their name of the soile where they were borne: for *Gigantes* signifieth the sons of the earth: the Aborigines, or (as Cesar calleth them) Indigenae; that is, born and bred out of the earth where they inhabited.[2]

Albion is the ancestral soil of England on which Blake stood and from which he sprang. He is also the titanic forefather of Blake's own hinterland of symbolism—the original 'Giant Form' composing the greater world of his inner life from which are derived the 'Zoas' or living creatures who make up the *dramatis personae* of the prophetic books. Historically, Albion is the dreamer whose dream is the vision of history or the circle of destiny, and morally, or in terms of human nature, he is the field of spiritual adventure for the race. Finally, he is the description of the origin and destiny—that is, the essential existence—of humanity.

[1] Milton, *History of Britain*, bk. I, chap. 1 (*Works*, New York: Columbia University Press, 1932, X, pp. 4 ff.). The reference is connected with the sons of Japhet after the flood and also with the derivation of a line of giants—which presumably included Albion—from some oceanic abode reminiscent of Atlantis. (Cf. Spenser, *The Faerie Queene*, IV, xi, 16–N.F.).

[2] Holinshed, *Chronicles*, London, 1807, I, chap. 3, p. 432.

The existence of humanity is an original form which includes the world of man's immediate environment. The immediate environment of an acorn planted as the seed of an oak is the earth. But if its form is to be completely described in terms of its possible destiny, the description must include that unplanted or 'unfallen' form of the original oak, appearing and disappearing within the realm of created nature.

> 'Whatever can be Created can be Annihilated: Forms cannot:
> The Oak is cut down by the Ax, the Lamb falls by the Knife,
> But their Forms Eternal Exist For-ever. Amen. Hallelujah!'[3]

The painter who attempts to paint the acorn in its plot of earth will be painting its 'portrait', but if he wishes to paint it 'historically'—in terms of its origin and its possible destiny—he will be obliged to paint an oak. Blake calls himself a 'History Painter', and his vision of human existence is the oak tree itself, the Giant Albion, the hero of the prophetic books. He is, however, careful to distinguish his vision from the rational abstractions of a philosopher of history. Albion is not merely the general concept of humanity: 'A History Painter Paints The Hero, & not Man in General, but most minutely in Particular'.[4] As the hero of this kind of history, Albion includes within himself all that man has been and can be, for he is the particular exemplar of man's origin and his possible destiny. In his fallen condition, he is, however, separated from the complete realization of his powers, represented by his 'emancipation' whose name is the name of a Christian's vision of the eternal city—Jerusalem.

Like Dante's Beatrice, Jerusalem partakes of this world and the next, and she is that part of Albion which remains separate only in his wandering away from eternal existence. Their reunion, therefore, is part of Albion's recognition that she is herself united to the 'Divine Image' as illustrated by the engraving at the end of the epic, *Jerusalem*. By this use of Albion and Jerusalem, Blake shows the change which has taken place in the relationship between the macrocosm, or the great world of nature, and the microcosm, or the little world of man. In this change of outlook, unfallen human existence becomes the macrocosm, and the natural field of experience the microcosm. If this is man's possible goal, it must be latent in his origin. Blake's expression of such an origin and its fulfilment takes the form of a movement from the original innocence of a Garden of Eden to the final experience of a New Jerusalem. The entire theme is foreshadowed in his *Songs of Innocence and Experience*, satirically corrected and sharpened in *The Marriage of Heaven and Hell*, symbolically tried and

---

[3] *Milton*, 35: 36–8. [Keynes, 32: 36–8, p. 522.]

[4] *Annotations to Reynolds's 'Discourses,'* p. 106. This vision goes beyond the appearances of nature and cannot be derived from them. Cf. Letter to Thomas Butts, Nov. 22, 1802: 'If you have not Nature before you for Every Touch, you cannot Paint Portrait: & if you have Nature before you at all, you cannot Paint History; it was Michael Angelo's opinion & is mine.'

proved in the minor prophecies, outlined in *The Four Zoas*, and completed in *Milton* and *Jerusalem*. Using his interpretation of the Bible from Genesis to Revelation as a model, he looks back to man's origin as to a garden newly planted and sown, and forward to his consummation as to a city 'prepared as a bride adorned for her husband' (Rev. xxi: 2). According to the fourfold method of interpreting scripture, Jerusalem is literally the earthly city, allegorically the body of the faithful, morally the believer, and anagogically the heavenly city of the Redeemed. As the bride or 'emanation' of the Giant Albion, Jerusalem is Blake's way of uniting the Christian tradition of an Englishman to the English inheritance of a Christian. . . .

Reprinted from *The Valley of Vision*, by Peter F. Fisher, edited by Northrop Frye, Toronto, 1961, pp. 220–3, by permission of University of Toronto Press. Copyright, Canada, 1961 by University of Toronto Press.

A Personal Influence

... It was then that the poetry of William Blake descended on me like an apocalypse. Tennyson had chimed in with moods, and shown me felicity. Blake shook me to the depths of my awakening mind, scattered the world of my objective vision, and left me floundering in subjective fantasy. I did not, at that time, venture far into the Prophetic Books; but the *Songs of Innocence and Experience,* and the poems from the Rossetti and Pickering manuscripts, pierced me like gleaming steel, and their meaning was annealed to my mind. Their meaning?— I should rather say their mystery, for many of these poems were not easy to understand, and indeed I did not seek to understand them. From the beginning I was content with the incantation of a poem, and I still maintain that this is the quality essential to poetry.

Blake kept his ascendency in my mind for many years—indeed, though I have submitted to many influences and have been fired to more than one enthusiasm in the intervening years, there is no poet with whom today I would more readily identify the poetic essence. For me, Blake is absolute. Shakespeare is richer, Milton is more sonorous, Hopkins more sensuous—one could make many more comparative statements; but Blake has no need of qualifying epithets: he is simply poetic, in imagination and in expression....

The Contrary Experience, Faber and Faber, London, 1963, p. 161. Reprinted by permission also of Horizon Press, copyright 1963.

The Vision of Innocence

William Blake's *Songs of Innocence* were engraved by 1789. Not until five years later were they incorporated into *The Songs of Innocence and Experience, Shewing the Two Contrary States of the Human Soul*. Partly because the *Songs of Innocence* have found their way into the nursery, partly because the *Songs of Experience* include some of Blake's most brilliant poems, there has been a tendency to discount the *Songs of Innocence* or to save them by reading them as highly ironic poems, each with its own built-in contraries. This produces strained readings and obscures the full import of Innocence as one of the 'two contrary states'. We must first take the *Songs of Innocence* in their own right, and by doing so we can make better sense of the *Songs of Experience*.

What the contrary states mean is shown in two poems Blake enclosed in letters to his friend and patron, Thomas Butts, the first on October 2, 1800, the second two years later, on November 22, 1802. In the first the themes of Innocence are restated in the language of vision. Blake achieves an ecstatic transcendence on the shore at Felpham and looks down upon his mortal Shadow and his wife's. His eyes 'Like a Sea without shore / Continue Expanding, / The Heavens commanding'. All Heaven becomes one man, Jesus, who purges away 'All my mire & my clay' (as in 'The Little Black Boy' or 'The Chimney Sweeper') and enfolds Blake in his bosom, saying:

> This is My Fold,
> O thou Ram horn'd with gold,
> Who awakest from Sleep
> On the Sides of the Deep.

The lion and the wolf, whose 'roarings resound', the 'loud Sea & deep gulf'—all of them threatening—now become, for Jesus, 'guards of My Fold'.

> And the voice faded mild.
> I remain'd as a Child;
> All I ever had known
> Before me bright Shone.

This draws together visionary perception and childlike innocence, and makes visionary transcendence a discovery of the protected world of

the divine sheepfold; where seeming evil is absorbed into a pastoral
version of Order.

In the second of these poems we encounter the trials of Experience.
Blake is torn with conflicting obligations; 'the duties of life each
other cross.'

> Must Flaxman look upon me as wild,
> And all my friends be with doubts beguil'd?

Blake resolves the conflict by defying the sun and looking through its
earthly form:

> Another Sun feeds our life's streams,
> We are not warmed with thy beams...
> My Mind is not with thy light array'd,
> Thy terrors shall not make me afraid.

The defiance makes all the natural world shrink and grieve, but
Blake moves forward with triumph into the world of vision:

> The Sun was hot
> With the bows of my Mind & the Arrows of Thought—
> My bowstring fierce with Ardour breathes,
> My arrows glow in their golden sheaves.

'Now,' he concludes, 'I a fourfold vision see ... Tis fourfold in my
supreme delight.' He has wrested vision from grief, and won through
to a trust in his powers (pp. 816-18). [The page references are to
G. Keynes's edition of Blake, Nonesuch, 1957 and O.U.P., 1966.]

The *Songs of Innocence* cultivate a tone of naïvety, but we must
recognize that what is spontaneously discovered by the child has in
fact been earned by the poet's visionary powers. It is not easy to
achieve Innocence, and one does not reach it by a simple process of
subtraction. While the *Songs of Innocence* insist upon the naïve vision,
they show, in their own way, as much calculation as the more radical
of Wordsworth's *Lyrical Ballads*. Wordsworth's subjects are children,
displaced persons or wanderers; humble people who live in dwellings
all but indistinguishable from nature; morally displaced persons such
as criminals and idiots—those rejected or oppressed by society; poets
as social misfits and dreamers; and, most generally, people who have
not entered and for some reason have fallen out of the social pattern.
Wordsworth's treatment of them is a bold assertion of the dignity of
their elementary feelings. Coleridge speaks of the 'daring humble-
ness' of Wordsworth's language and versification, and we know that
their challenge was felt and resisted by early critics. Blake's *Songs of
Innocence* are more traditional in their literary and religious associa-
tions and more remote from such stubborn commonplaces of life as
swelling ankles, idiot sons, and the love of property. But, like Words-
worth's poems, and, in fact, like most pastorals, they create a vision

that risks one-sidedness. Such a vision teeters on the verge of calling to mind all it excludes, and Blake has given us what Innocence excludes in the *Songs of Experience*. But pastoral can teeter without falling into overt irony, and its assertion is all the more defiant for that poise.

The defiance is the poet's. The innocents themselves remain indifferent to all that crowds in upon us. This indifference is not ignorance, any more than it is in Wordsworth's 'We Are Seven', where the child insists that her dead brother and sister are still in the midst of their family. The childlike trust becomes a metaphor for the more strenuous faith and defiance of doubt that all may achieve.

The landscape of Innocence is a fostering, humanized landscape. It echoes human songs and laughter; it accepts and sympathizes with every feeling. The 'Laughing Song' is one of the simplest of the *Songs*, but Wordsworth found it worth copying into his commonplace book in 1804. It closes with the invitation to participate:

> When the painted birds laugh in the shade,
> Where our table with cherries and nuts is spread,
> Come live & be merry, and join with me,
> To sing the sweet chorus of 'Ha, Ha, He'.

The language is somewhat archaic ('painted birds'), the form reminiscent of Elizabethan lyrics, and the poem closes tellingly with the call to 'sing the sweet chorus'. The harmony of shepherds (the song first appears written in a copy of *Poetical Sketches* as *Sung ... by a Young Shepherd*) and maids, of man and nature, is caught in the very meaningless exultation of the 'Ha, Ha, He'. If one calls it witless exultation, one has only underlined the point: this is the least self-conscious of sounds, the pure merry note. So it is with 'Spring'. Animal sounds, 'infant noise', and the sounding flute are all part of one song; and child and lamb play together with no sense of difference. Music is only one manifestation of the reciprocal warmth that marks all relationships (every creature is related to every other); the nurse is trustful and indulgent, old John on the echoing green participates in the laughter of the children at play. There is neither jealousy nor restriction; darkness brings safe repose and satiation. The 'happy Blossom' welcomes both the merry sparrow and the sobbing robin, rejoicing in its power to accept or comfort each alike.

In 'The Lamb', the harmony grows out of a deeper union:

> I a child, & thou a lamb,
> We are called by his name.

Each creature is a member one of another because of their common membership in God's love and the body of His creation. This participation in one life is nicely stated in 'The Shepherd', where the freedom of the shepherd ('From the morn to the evening he strays')

is consonant with his watchfulness, for he is himself a sheep watched
over by his Shepherd with generous love. The condition of peace is
security without restraint. The participation is extended in 'The Divine
Image' to 'every man of every clime', for every man—'heathen, turk,
or jew'—is 'Man, his child and care'.

In 'Night' all these themes come together. The moon sits in
'heaven's high bower' like the happy blossom. The darkening fields are
left by sleeping lambs to the 'feet of angels bright'. As in *Paradise
Lost,*

> Millions of spiritual Creatures walk the Earth
> Unseen, both when we wake, and when we sleep
> ...oft in bands
> While they keep watch, a nightly rounding walk
> With Heav'nly touch of instrumental sounds
> In full harmonic number join'd, their songs
> Divide the night, and lift our thoughts to Heaven
> (IV, 677–78, 684–88).

Blake's world of Innocence is not, however, Paradise. The angels
cannot always control wolves and tigers, or deny them victims; but the
victims are received, 'New worlds to inherit'.

> And there the lion's ruddy eyes
> Shall flow with tears of gold,
> And pitying the tender cries,
> And walking round the fold,
> Saying 'Wrath, by his meekness,
> And by his health, sickness
> Is driven away
> From our immortal day.
>
> And now beside thee, bleating lamb,
> I can lie down and sleep;
> Or think on him who bore thy name,
> Graze after thee and weep.
> For, wash'd in life's river,
> My bright mane for ever
> Shall shine like the gold
> As I guard o'er the fold' (33-48).

The regeneration of the lion, so that he can now 'remain always in
Paradise', is a perhaps unconscious but eloquent reply to Mandeville's
comment on Milton. As the angels pitied the howling wolves and
tigers, the lion can now pity the tender cries of the sheep. It is a
splendid assertion of the power of meekness, as the gold of the lion's
'bright mane' becomes an aureole.

But pastoral celebration does not contain all that Blake wishes to
say. 'The School Boy', while it seems spoken in trust of parents'
understanding, is a lament against restriction. It is one of the poems

that await the coming into existence of the *Songs of Experience,*
where, five years later, it was placed. Other poems are less clear cases.
'Holy Thursday' presents the Ascension Day 'anniversary' of the
charity school children. The 'grey-headed beadles' who lead the chil-
dren into St Paul's are mentioned first, and they may seem like threat-
ening figures with their 'wands white as snow'. But the children flow
like a river, they are like flowers, they have a 'radiance all their own',
and they raise their choral voice 'like a mighty wind' or 'like harmo-
nious thunderings the seats of Heavens among'. And, as is usual in
these poems, the closing lines have gained meaning from the whole
poem. Now the formidable beadles take their place below the angelic
children:

> Beneath them sat the aged men, wise guardians of the poor;
> Then cherish pity, lest you drive an angel from your door.

The last line seems pat and inadequate to those who are on the watch
for irony; yet it converts the aged men to the counterparts of Abraham
and Lot, who entertained angels at their door and were shown favour.

In 'The Little Black Boy' the pain of being born with a different face
is genuine and acute. Blake enters imaginatively into the condition of
the boy and his mother. She supplies a consoling vision that makes the
suffering temporary and even a source of pride. By showing her boy
that the body is a 'cloud' that absorbs the beams of God's love and
vanishes after a short term of trial, she turns upside down the stan-
dards of the world around him. This can save his sense of worth. His
body is better adapted than the white boy's to bearing God's love
(God is here conceived much as in Milton, where He dwells in 'un-
approached light' which the angels can bear to behold only when they
veil their eyes with their wings). And all bodies are the instruments by
which we are trained to live in the spirit.

The poem ends with a reversal like the one that sets the ominous
beadles below the angelic children of 'Holy Thursday'. The little
black boy sees himself with the English child in heaven:

> I'll shade him from the heat, till he can bear
> To lean in joy upon our father's knee;
> And then I'll stand and stroke his silver hair,
> And be like him, and he will then love me.

One can see pathos, surely, in the fundamental desire to 'be like him'
—the lack of any image of oneself that can give repose or self-respect.
Yet there is also a strain of mature understanding or even pity in the
recognition that the white boy can bear less love and can give less
love—that he needs to wait for the black boy to be like him before he
can recognize their oneness in a common father. We may deplore the
comparative quietism of this, but we must recognize a faith that per-
mits the boy to live with the inevitable without surrendering to it.

'The Chimney Sweeper' descends farther into suffering, and the plight of the sweeps is as grim as can be conceived. What the poem is saying, nevertheless, is that the naïve faith we see in Tom's dream is the means of survival. In a 'Song by an Old Shepherd' Blake had written:

> Blow, boisterous wind, stern winter frown,
> Innocence is a winter's gown;
> So clad, we'll abide life's pelting storm
> That makes our limbs quake, if our hearts be warm (64).

The chimney sweep, Tom, dreams that thousands of sweepers are 'lock'd up in coffins of black', when

> ... by came an Angel who had a bright key,
> And he open'd the coffins & set them all free;
> Then down a green plain leaping, laughing, they run,
> And wash in a river, and shine in the Sun.

The Angel is like those in 'Night' who receive the wolves' victims, 'New worlds to inherit'. Here the new world is the miserable child's vision of a heaven—green plains, a river to wash in, sunlight, play, a father. The old world is still there when Tom awakens, but Tom and his companions have a 'winter's gown':

> Tho' the morning was cold, Tom was happy & warm;
> So if all do their duty they need not fear harm.

The last line stings with irony as we think of the duties left unperformed by the boys' elders, and it has pathos if we take it to imply that Tom expects virtue to be rewarded in the world. But it is also a daring assertion of naïve faith, the faith that will inevitably be rewarded in its own terms, with an assurance of spirit that can transcend its worldly conditions. This naïve faith has both the precariousness and the strength of a pastoral vision: it seems too fragile to survive suffering, yet it somehow does survive, more vivid and intense than the world it transcends.

I have spoken of these assertions as metaphors for adult existence, and we can see their counterpart in Blake's letters:

> ... now I have lamented over the dead horse let me laugh & be merry with my friends till Christmas, for as Man liveth not by bread alone, I shall live altho' I should want bread—nothing is necessary to me but to do my Duty & to rejoice in the exceeding joy that is always poured on my Spirit (To William Hayley, October 7th, 1803).
> ... as none on Earth can give me Mental Distress, & I know that all Distress inflicted by Heaven is a Mercy, a Fig for all corporeal! Such Distress is My mock & scorn (To Thos. Butts, September 11th, 1801).

In 'The Little Girl Lost' and 'The Little Girl Found' we come to
the borderland between Innocence and Experience. Blake moved these
poems from one group to the other, and this convertibility helps us
understand the relationship of 'contrary states'. In the two border
poems, the seeming forces of evil prove to be as gentle and fostering as
parents—perhaps through the influence of the sleeping maid, whose
innocence creates a precinct of 'hallow'd ground'. The lion's 'ruby
tears' flow with pity for her unprotectedness: her weakness and her
trust disarm the beasts of prey. In the second poem the lion reveals an
angel within, and his cave becomes a palace; the parents who brave
the wilds for the sake of their lost child are rewarded with a new
freedom and security:

> To this day they dwell
> In a lonely dell;
> Nor fear the wolvish howl
> Nor the lions' growl.

They live in a world where evil has no power, however it may seem to
threaten others.

If we stress the faith that is strong enough to transcend the power
of the world, these poems clearly fall into the pattern of Innocence.
If, on the other hand, we stress the adversity to be overcome and the
courage with which it is faced, they move toward Experience, although
they remain the most triumphant of the *Songs of Experience*. Seven-
year-old Lyca wanders into the 'desart wild' and is lost. Significantly,
she is concerned not for herself but for her parents' grief. She con-
fidently summons the moon to guard her and goes to sleep. The beasts
of the wild play around her body, licking her and weeping with pity,
until at last they accept her as one of themselves, loose her dress, and
carry her to their caves. In 'The Little Girl Found' we see that
Lyca's parents do indeed grieve and search for her (as parents in
Innocence do). After seven days of anxiety and distress, the mother
can go no farther and is carried in her husband's arms. They too
encounter a lion, which seems to stalk them. But suddenly he licks
their hands and becomes a 'Spirit arm'd in gold' (like the lion in
'Night'). He leads them to his palace where Lyca lies sleeping among
'tygers wild'.

The strength of Experience comes of its ability to sustain or recover
the faith of Innocence. The state of Experience is one of suffering, but
we have already seen much of that in Innocence. More significant is
the attitude taken toward suffering: those who are frustrated and
corrupted by it, surrender; those who seek their freedom and keep
their vision alive, rebel. In some poems only the condition of suffering
is given: these contribute to that composite image, the contrary of the
pastoral vision of Innocence, of a world to be met with either despair
or defiance. In 'A Little Girl Lost', Ona is terrified by the father whose

'loving look' is the face of the punitive moralist, professing (sincerely
enough) anxiety for his straying child, but scarcely concealing the
self-pity of the rigid law-maker. In 'A Little Boy Lost' the Cordelia-
like protestations of the boy lead to his torture and murder by the
priests.

In other poems the surrender is clear. In 'The Angel' and 'My
Pretty Rose Tree', life is rejected for the sake of chastity or possessive-
ness; and the result is armed fear or resentment. The 'Nurse's Song'
is the expression of anxiety and envy; the repressive nurse is project-
ing doubts of her own self into the lives of the children. In 'The Sick
Rose', the secrecy of love becomes disease. The 'crimson joy' suggests
the rose's complicity both in passion and in secrecy: disguise destroys
from within. We see this more clearly in 'The Lilly', where the modest
rose and the humble sheep protect themselves with a thorn and a
threatening horn; whereas the lily's open delight in love makes her
whiteness incapable of stain, as is the case with Oothoon later in the
Visions of the Daughters of Albion.

The central distinction between honest wrath and stifled or cor-
rupted energy is given in the opening poems of the *Songs of Experi-
ence*. 'Introduction' announces the visionary Bard

> Whose ears have heard
> The Holy Word
> That walk'd among the ancient trees,
>
> Calling the lapsed Soul,
> And weeping in the evening dew;
> That might controll
> The starry pole,
> And fallen, fallen light renew! (3-10).

'Controll' here still carries the sense of 'contradict' or 'disprove'. The
Holy Word is the Poetic Genius within man summoning the dawn of
revived life. 'Earth's Answer' comes out of 'grey despair'; Earth's locks
are as gray as those of the virgin who resists love in 'The Angel'. She
can see only the God she has created for herself:

> Prison'd on wat'ry shore,
> Starry Jealousy does keep my den:
> Cold and hoar,
> Weeping o'er,
> I hear the Father of the ancient men.
>
> Selfish father of men!
> Cruel, jealous, selfish fear!
> Can delight,
> Chain'd in night,
> The virgins of youth and morning bear? (6-15).

Are we to take Earth's words as a just condemnation of the Holy Word,

or is Earth's despair the counterpart of the resentment of Adam and
Eve in their fallen state, before they recover the power to love and
recognize that their Judge is also their Redeemer? The latter seems the
more plausible.

'The Tyger' is the best known of Blake's songs and the most fre-
quently and elaborately interpreted. The phrase 'fearful symmetry'—
whatever its possible symbolic suggestions—is clearly the initial
puzzle: the 'symmetry' implies an ordering hand or intelligence, the
'fearful' throws doubt on the benevolence of the Creator. The 'forests
of the night' are the darkness out of which the tiger looms, brilliant in
contrast; they also embody the doubt or confusion that surrounds the
origins of the tiger. In the case of 'The Lamb', the Creator 'calls him-
self a Lamb. / He is meek, & he is mild; / He became a little child'.
In 'The Tyger' the Creator again is like what he creates, and the form
that must be supplied him now is the Promethean smith working
violently at his forge. The last alteration we have of this much altered
poem insists upon the likeness of Creator and created: 'What dread
hand Form'd thy dread feet?' The tiger is an image of the Creator;
its 'deadly terrors' must be His.

The most puzzling stanza of the poem is the next-to-last:

> When the stars threw down their spears,
> And water'd heaven with their tears,
> Did he smile his work to see?
> Did he who made the Lamb make thee?

The first two lines are the crux of the poem. Are the tears the rage of
the defeated, or the tears of mercy as in a later Notebook poem,
'Morning'?

> To find the Western path
> Right thro' the Gates of Wrath
> I urge my way;
> Sweet Mercy leads me on:
> With soft repentant moan
> I see the break of day.
>
> The war of swords & spears
> Melted by dewy tears
> Exhales on high;
> The sun is freed from fears
> And with soft grateful tears
> Ascends the sky (421).

Here we have come through wrath to mercy, through night to dawn.
This progression appears again in *Jerusalem*, where Los, the imagina-
tive power, considers his task as visionary poet. Los is seeking to make
error visible so that it may be thrown off, and his satiric task requires
him to adopt the 'forms of cruelty'.

> I took the sighs & tears & bitter groans,
> I lifted them into my Furnaces to form the spiritual sword
> That lays open the hidden heart. I drew forth the pang
> Of sorrow red hot: I work'd it on my resolute anvil...
> I labour day and night. I behold the soft affections
> Condense beneath my hammer into forms of cruelty,
> But still I labour in hope; tho' still my tears flow down:
> That he who will not defend Truth may be compell'd to defend
> A Lie: that he may be snared and caught and snared and taken:
> That Enthusiasm and Life may not cease...
>   (9:17-20, 26-31).

The 'spiritual sword / That lays open the hidden heart' is a counter-part of the tiger we see in the *Songs of Experience*. The wrath serves the ultimate end of redemption and becomes one with mercy. If the God of apparent wrath is also the God of forgiveness, the tiger's form is only superficially 'fearful'. In the words of Pope:

> Nor God alone in the still calm we find,
> He mounts the storm, and walks upon the wind
>   (*Essay on Man*, II, 109-10).

'The Tyger' dramatizes the terrors of the shocked doubter, but it moves with assurance—in the stanza I have quoted—to an assertion of faith (faith in the oneness of God, in the goodness of wrath, in the holiness of prophetic rage). When the last stanza repeats the first, but for the alteration of 'could' to 'dare', the question has been answered. The inconceivable of the first stanza has become the majestic certainty of the last: the daring of the Creator—whether God or man—is the cleansing wrath of the tiger.

The honest wrath that is celebrated in 'The Tyger' is the open and healthy response to suffering. In contrast, as we have seen, is the tortured brooding of the bound infant who sulks upon his mother's breast, or the viciousness that comes of 'unacted desires' in 'A Poison Tree'. In 'London' this pattern of externally imposed suppression (the swaddling bands of the infant, the binding with briars by priests in black gowns) or internal self-imposed repression (the armed fears of the virgin, the secret love of the rose) becomes a general condition whose meaning is evident only to the visionary poet. He alone sees and hears what others take for granted.

> In every cry of every Man,
> In every Infant's cry of fear,
> In every voice, in every ban,
> The mind-forg'd manacles I hear.

The power to penetrate the conventional sounds—whether street cries, oaths, infants' wails—makes the self-imposed tortures of man not simply audible but visible. The cry of the soot-covered chimney sweeper appalls—blackens as much as shocks, convicts as much as arouses—'every black'ning Church' (blackening with the guilt of its indifference far more than with soot). So too the 'hapless Soldier's sigh' brands the palace he has been suffering to defend with the guilt of causing his pain; and—sound made visible—'Runs in blood down Palace walls'.

> But most thro' midnight streets I hear
> How the youthful Harlot's curse
> Blasts the new born Infant's tear,
> And blights with plagues the Marriage hearse.

The visible stain has become a virulent infection, and its power is caught in the terrible poetic condensation that sees the marriage coach as already a hearse. The existence of the youthful harlot (another conventional street sound, as she curses in the night) is more than a source of physical infection; it is a symptom of the moral disease evident only to the visionary poet. Except for his, there is no open rebellion in this London, no deeply felt outrage. Each cry or sigh or curse arises from a single individual's grief. Only the poet hears what is *in* each cry or sees *how* it looks and acts—in short, what it means. The gap between the suffering and the awareness is part of the terror of the London Blake presents; it is made all the sharper if we contrast the isolated suffering of these cries with the echoing responsiveness on the village green of Innocence.

Only when we grant Innocence its proper value does the full dialectical force of the two contrary states become clear. We can see the potential suffering that surrounds the world of Innocence and the potential triumph that Experience permits. Blake is less concerned with exposing injustice than with finding a vital response to it. The evil he presents is in each case the denial of life, whether imposed from without by society or made within by the individual. The good he espouses is the life-giving vision, whether serenely enjoyed or indignantly defended. Clearly serene transcendence of evil is seldom possible although, as we have seen, Blake rejoices in such moments. And Innocence, like Experience, has its false aspect as well as its true.

In the manuscript of *The Four Zoas* Blake made this note: 'Unorganiz'd Innocence: An Impossibility. Innocence dwells with Wisdom, but never with Ignorance' (380). Wisdom need not imply self-consciousness or acquaintance with evil, any more than it does for Adam in Milton's Paradise. But in the years that intervened between the first engraving of the *Songs of Innocence* in 1789 and their yoking to the new *Songs of Experience* in 1793, Blake explored the varieties of false Innocence, which is a denial of life rather than a confident assertion of its goodness.

In *Tiriel* (1789) we encounter a seeming contrast that at last becomes an identity. Tiriel is the tyrannical father who enslaves his sons until they rebel and cast him out. Tyrant and slave are correlative terms; the slave rebels in order to become a tyrant in turn. Tiriel wanders, a bitter and blind outcast, to the Edenic vales of Har. Here we encounter the first reversal. Har and Heva are 'like two children' tended by their aged nurse, Mnetha, and they prattle with childish innocence as they greet Tiriel. It is not until the third section of the poem that Har and Heva reveal their own great age, greater than Tiriel's. They vaguely recognize him from a past they only dimly retain; he conceals his identity, and they are entirely absorbed in the pleasures of the present:

'Thou shalt not go,' said Heva, 'till thou hast seen our singing birds
And heard Har sing in the great cage & slept upon our fleeces'
                                                    (3:22-3).

But Tiriel is moved by 'madness and deep dismay' to leave, and Har and Heva 'soon forgot their tears' in the simplicity of timeless childhood.

Tiriel next meets his brother, Ijim, an embodiment of wildness and superstition. Ijim sees only a spectral fiend in Tiriel rather than the brother who has been a tyrant. Ijim brings Tiriel back to his palace under force, boasting to Tiriel's sons that he has enslaved his elusive demon in the disguise of Tiriel. When the sons claim to recognize Tiriel, Ijim goes off, unconvinced, returning to the 'secret forests' where he can nurse his gloomy fears. Ijim is one of the products of Tiriel's tyranny—the Natural Man, more beast than man, full of strength but childlike in superstitious terror.

Tiriel now curses his children and brings death on all of them except Hela, his daughter, whom he forces to lead him back to the pleasures of Har and Heva. Hela hates her father's cruelty; she rebels helplessly until he curses her too and drives her mad. Finally, they reach the vales of Har and Heva, where Tiriel defies the protective Mnetha: 'Lead me to Har and Heva; I am Tiriel, King of the west.'

At this point comes the second reversal. For Tiriel now identifies Har as his father:

'O weak mistaken father of a lawless race,
Thy laws, O Har, & Tiriel's wisdom, end together in a
curse' (8:7-8).

Tiriel further identifies Har as the source of all the evil his own life has exemplified. Har, dawdling in his earthly paradise, an ancient infant, is the source of rigid law, the teacher of the ways of the Natural Man and of subtle hypocrisy: 'And now,' Tiriel concludes, 'my paradise is fall'n & a drear sandy plain / Returns my thirsty hissings in a curse on thee, O Har.' Tiriel dies with his curse. This is the third reversal: the arrested earthly paradise of the superannuated pseudo-innocent is the source of the cycle of frustration and aggression, of slave and tyrant, that Tiriel's own life has made clear. Once he has slain his sons, Tiriel is ready to return to these peaceful vales; but he arrives only to curse his father in turn.

This poem is Blake's first dramatic presentation of a 'negative' State, the mock order of spurious innocence. It is not a condemnation of Innocence itself, but rather an exposure of its use as a disguise. The reversals that run through the poem move stage by stage toward the final equation of the illusion of Innocence (which the self-righteous achieve by self-deception) with the repressive and debasing tyranny of Tiriel. The garden becomes a desert at the close, and the details of Har's great cage and the fleeces on which he lies become more obviously sinister. Tiriel complains that he has been

> Compell'd to pray repugnant & to humble the immortal spirit
> Till I am subtil as a serpent in a paradise,
> Consuming all, both flowers & fruits, insects & warbling birds
> (8:36-8).

Beyond the poem's cycles of repression and tyranny lies the memory of the 'immortal spirit'. Tiriel cannot revive it in himself; but he can at last come to recognize its absence from both Har's laws and his own 'wisdom'.

In *The Book of Thel* (1789) Blake gives us a new version of false Innocence—false here because it seeks withdrawal rather than transcendence and falls into the aimless round of passivity rather than pay the cost of living by the 'immortal spirit'. At the close of the poem the maiden Thel flees 'back unhinder'd' to the vales of Har, where she can accept the prison of passive infancy in an earthly paradise.

Thel is troubled at the outset. She laments her mortality and transiency in images that have a telltale softness and mild charm:

> Ah! Thel is like a wat'ry bow, and like a parting cloud;
> Like a reflection in a glass; like shadows in the water;
> Like dreams of infants, like a smile upon an infant's face;
> Like the dove's voice; like transient day; like music in the air
> (1:8-11).

There follow three dialogues, each with a creature more lowly and transient than herself; and each reveals what Thel painfully lacks—a sense of function, an ability to give oneself, and to trust in being received and rewarded with love in turn. The Lily of the Valley, small and humble, feeds the cropping Lamb and revives the cattle with its perfume—'Giving to those that cannot crave, the voiceless, the o'ertired' (33). And the Lily of the Valley in turn hears with the candid faith of true Innocence, the voice of God:

> Saying, 'Rejoice, thou humble grass, thou new-born lilly flower,
> Thou gentle maid of silent valleys and of modest brooks;
> For thou shalt be clothed in light, and fed with morning manna,
> Till summer's heat melts thee beside the fountains and the springs
> To flourish in eternal vales ... (1:21-5).

The Cloud, too, is transient. It vanishes into the springs from which animals drink; it weds the 'fair-eyed dew'

Till we arise link'd in a golden band and never part,
But walk united, bearing food to all our tender flowers
　(3:15-16).

Thel's life is without service in the vales of Har; she encounters all life around her as a pleasure of the senses but not as a true confrontation ('I hear the warbling birds, / But I feed not the warbling birds; they fly and seek their food'). She speaks in self-pity of having no use unless it be at death to become 'the food of worms'. To this the Cloud replies in a tone that is sharp and therapeutic:

Then if thou art the food of worms, O virgin of the skies,
How great thy use, how great thy blessing! Every thing that lives
Lives not alone nor for itself ... (3:25-7).

But when Thel encounters the Worm, all the stereotypes of sentimental pity return:

Is this a Worm? I see thee lay helpless & naked, weeping,
And none to answer, none to cherish thee with mother's smiles
　(4:5-6).

At once the Clod of Clay appears, as full of protective solicitude as the mothers of the *Songs of Innocence,* and not without reproach: 'O beauty of the vales of Har! we live not for ourselves.'

Thel cannot learn the lesson of Innocence. The Clod of Clay is the bride of God, the mother of His children, and, like Milton's Adam in Paradise, can feel that she is happier than she knows:

But how this is, sweet maid, I know not, and I cannot know;
I ponder, and I cannot ponder; yet I live and love
　(5:5-6).

The Clod of Clay does not need to question and to seek assurances; she gives herself completely and trusts the value of what she is and does. All these creatures are taken in love, wedded to all other creatures and to God in those creatures—as the child and the lamb are one in Jesus.

When Thel at last is brought to contemplate her place in the one life that all these creatures enjoy, she can only see—in vision—'her own grave plot', and hear a 'voice of sorrow breathed from the hollow pit'. What is revealed to her is what Blake had cancelled from Tiriel's last speech—an account of the life of formal law and inner repression. Tiriel had put it:

　　　　　Some close shut up
In silent deceit, poisons inhaling from the morning rose,
With daggers hid beneath their lips & poison in their tongue;
Or eyed with little sparks of Hell, or with infernal brands

Flinging flames of discontent & plagues of dark despair;
Or those whose mouths are graves, whose teeth the gates of eternal
   death.
Can wisdom be put in a silver rod, or love in a golden bowl?
Is the son of a king warmed without wool or does he cry with a voice
Of thunder? does he look upon the sun & laugh or stretch
His little hands into the depths of the sea, to bring forth
The deadly cunning of the scaly tribe & spread it to the morning?
   (8:12-22).

So here, the voice of sorrow that Thel hears—the voice of her own
anxieties—reveals all the horror of malice, vindictiveness, hypocrisy,
pain. These appear as the life of the senses, and the last of them is
the repressiveness of sexual chastity:

Why cannot the Ear be closed to its own destruction?
Or the glist'ning Eye to the poison of a smile?
Why are Eyelids stor'd with arrows ready drawn,
Where a thousand fighting men in ambush lie?
Or an Eye of gifts & graces show'ring fruits & coined gold?
Why a Tongue impress'd with honey from every wind?
Why an Ear, a whirlpool fierce to draw creations in?
Why a Nostril wide inhaling terror, trembling, & affright?
Why a tender curb upon the youthful burning boy?
Why a little curtain of flesh on the bed of our desire?
   (6:11-20).

This is the trial set in the *Songs of Experience,* the suffering imposed
from without and within by life in the world. It is the occasion for
either a lapse into Selfhood or a transcendent return to that Innocence
by which this life is judged. Thel's faith fails her, and she flees with
a shriek, back to the vales of Har.

Thel's false Innocence defines the true Innocence of the humbler
creatures. Her self-consciousness may be the inevitable cost of being
human, but her refusal to attempt to transcend it in the annihilation of
Selfhood and the triumph of the 'immortal spirit' becomes a failure of
humanity. She will have the comfort of the aged nurse, Mnetha, in-
stead of the dignity of true existence. Blake is defending Innocence by
distinguishing it from its worldly imitation, which becomes—as we
have seen—a life of passive sensuousness rather than of active exer-
tions of the spirit. We may do well to remember Bernard Shaw's
Blakean vision of Hell, where the Devil is a courtly aesthete who cannot
bear very much reality. To put wisdom 'in a silver rod, or love in a
golden bowl' is to convert the energies of the spirit to works of precious
lifelessness and specious orderliness, things of merely worldly value.

The *Visions of the Daughters of Albion* (1793) carries the problem
of Innocence a stage further. The three central figures are the daring
virgin, Oothoon; her tortured and indecisive lover, Theotormon; and
the brutal ravisher and moralist, Bromion. They appear to be charac-

ters, but, as each speaks out of a consciousness that is deep and in-
clusive, each becomes a 'State'—a mode of vision and an appropriate
world view. At the close of the poem, their relationship has become a
fixed one of endless repetition:

> Thus every morning wails Oothoon; but Theotormon sits
> Upon the margin'd ocean conversing with shadows dire
> (8:11–12).

When Oothoon turns to Theotormon with frankly avowed love,
defying moral conventions, Bromion rends her 'with his thunders',
stamps her with his signet as an owner does his slave, possesses her as
the English tyrant does the 'soft American plains', and offers her to
Theotormon as his discarded and pregnant harlot. There is an
anomaly in Bromion's rage; it is as much a rage of moral vindictive-
ness as of sexual possession. Bromion's rage is what makes Oothoon, in
others' eyes—even in her own at first—a harlot; it is the open assertion
of power, of a lawgiver more than a lover. As Oothoon calls down the
self-punishment of bewildered remorse, her lover Theotormon
'severely smiles' without turning to her. Oothoon has the strength to
win through to trust in her immortal spirit; and she tries in turn to
awaken Theotormon to life:

> I cry: arise, O Theotormon! for the village dog
> Barks at the breaking day: the nightingale has done lamenting;
> The lark does rustle in the ripe corn, and the Eagle returns
> From nightly prey and lifts his golden beak to the pure east,
> Shaking the dust from his immortal pinions to awake
> The sun that sleeps too long. Arise, my Theotormon, I am pure,
> Because the night is gone that clos'd me in its deadly black
>   (2:23-9).

But, for Theotormon, 'the night and morn / Are both alike; a night of
sighs, a morning of fresh tears.'

Oothoon tries to bring Theotormon to a perception that sees through
the surfaces of the given world. All creatures act from some power
that is deeper and greater than the five senses, whether instinct or
reminiscence. Each creature has its characteristic nature, and this can-
not be altered or debased. The annihilation of Selfhood is what
Oothoon has attained, and it must be distinguished from defilement:

> Sweetest the fruit that the worm feeds on, & the soul prey'd on by
>   woe,
> The new wash'd lamb ting'd with the village smoke, & the bright
>   swan
> By the red earth of our immortal river (3:17-19).

Blake carries over from *The Book of Thel* the distinction between the
virgin's withdrawal and the holiness of participation in a common life
and reciprocal use.

Theotormon's reply is only the lamentation of doubt. He is terrified by the unbounded:

> Where goest thou, O thought? to what remote land is thy flight?
> If thou returnest to the present moment of affliction
> Wilt thou bring comforts on thy wings, and dews and honey and
>   balm,
> Or poison from the desart wilds, from the eyes of the envier?
>   (4:8-11).

Bromion, in turn, clings to the visible world. It exists for the delight of a remote deity, 'spread in the infinite microscope'; and it receives from that deity a single kind of lawful existence. Bromion's world is one of sensuous gratification sanctioned by religious authority, governed by a worldly but priestly code:

> Ah! are there other wars beside the wars of sword and fire?
> And are there other sorrows beside the sorrows of poverty?
> And are there other joys beside the joys of riches and ease?
> And is there not one law for both the lion and the ox?
> And is there not eternal fire and eternal chains
> To bind the phantoms of existence from eternal life?
>   (4:19-24).

Once Bromion's vision is set forth, Oothoon can recognize its meaning. She sees Urizen, the rational lawgiver, in Bromion, and she repudiates the rigid law that rejects the facts of individual existence: 'How can one joy absorb another? Are not different joys / Holy, eternal, infinite? and each joy is a love' (5:5-6). Oothoon's lament opens out into a defence of the full complexity true order must attain:

> How can the giver of gifts experience the delights of the merchant?
> How the industrious citizen the pains of the husbandman?
> How different far the fat fed hireling with hollow drum,
> Who buys whole corn fields into wastes, and sings upon the heath!
> How different their eye and ear! how different the world to them!
>   (5:12-16).

The false order surrounds man with 'cold floods of abstraction' and 'forests of solitude', that is, isolates him in Selfhood; it imposes a specious structure of 'castles and high spires, where kings & priests may dwell'. Love is therein made to submit to 'spells of law' which bind the wife to 'one she loaths', as Oothoon is bound to Bromion by Theotormon's fearful doubts. The 'castles and high spires' are created in Theotormon's mind out of his cowardice; he creates mind-forged 'kings & priests'. The result is the dissembling of 'subtil modesty', the 'knowing, artful, secret, fearful, cautious, trembling hypocrite'. If such a world were real, Oothoon would be a whore, 'the crafty slave of selfish holiness'; but she is in fact 'a virgin fill'd with virgin fancies,/ Open to joy and to delight where ever beauty appears' (6:21-2).

Theotormon's way is a mock order of secrecy, masturbatory fanta-sies ('Where the horrible darkness is impressed with reflections of desire'), the 'self enjoyings of self denial', like Pope's Cave of Spleen, where the repressed energies of prudes explode in libidinous dreams or overt madness. Oothoon's way is tolerant acceptance of 'wanton play / In lovely copulation', 'the heaven of generous love'. The conflict lies between self-love and self-surrender:

Such is self-love that envies all, a creeping skeleton
With lamplike eyes watching around the frozen marriage bed
    (7:21-2).

Oothoon will catch for Theotormon 'girls of mild silver, or of furious gold'. This imagery of living silver and gold recalls the contrast in Milton of the spiritual treasures of Heaven to the visible splendours of Pandemonium. Blake draws a similar contrast between golden light and hoarded wealth:

Where the cold miser spreads his gold; or does the bright cloud drop
On his stone threshold? does his eye behold the beam that brings
Expansion to the eye of pity? (8:1-3).

His final image is one of energy transcending material bounds or making of matter its mere outward adornment:

The sea fowl takes the wintry blast for a cov'ring to her limbs,
And the wild snake the pestilence to adorn him with gems & gold;
And trees & birds & beasts & men behold their eternal joy
    (8:6-8).

Oothoon asserts an order of charity ('Arise, and drink your bliss, for every thing that lives is holy!') which is wedded to the energies of the flesh—only to their energies, it must be repeated, not to a life bounded by the senses or 'the wheel of false desire'. Here the improvement of sensual enjoyment becomes the means of achieving spiritual freedom in the body; the freedom of love makes the body its instrument with-out any outward limit set to its spontaneous joy. The order of mind which, for Bromion, has rationalized the order of the flesh and made it systematic is the enemy to be subdued, for it is the denial of the spirit and of charity. Theotormon's fear of his unvoiced desires makes him suppress them; he has neither the 'insolent confidence' of a systematic thinker, nor the freedom from others' moral systems that Oothoon attains. The poem is a splendid attack upon the repressive nature of moral legalism, and on all those false orders that become a denial of spirit—that is, of the order of charity.

From 'Blake: Vision and Satire', in *To the Palace of Wisdom: Studies in Order and Energy from Dryden to Blake*. New York, 1964, pp. 390–410. Copyright © 1964 by Martin Price. Reprinted by permission of Doubleday and Company, Inc.

Select Bibliography

BLAKE'S ILLUMINATED BOOKS

These are the libraries and museums where the original copies of Blake's Illuminated Books can be seen:
British Museum, London; Fitzwilliam Museum, Cambridge; Bodleian Library, Oxford; Melbourne Art Gallery, Australia; Auckland Public Library, New Zealand. In USA: Lessing J. Rosenwald Collection, Library of Congress, Washington, DC; Pierpont Morgan Library, New York; New York Public Library; Harvard College Library, Cambridge, Mass.; Yale University Library, New Haven, Conn.

FACSIMILES

These excellent colour facsimiles of Blake's Illuminated Books, published by the Blake Trust and the Trianon Press in limited editions of between 400 and 800 copies, can be seen in many University Libraries:

Jerusalem (1951); *Songs of Innocence* (1954); *Songs of Innocence and Experience* (1955); *Urizen* (1958); *Visions of Daughters of Albion* (1959); *Marriage of Heaven and Hell* (1960); *America* (1963); *Thel* (1965); *Milton* (1967); *Europe* (1969); *All Religions are One* (1970). In black and white: *Jerusalem* (1953); *The Gates of Paradise* (1968).

COLLECTED WRITINGS

Writings of William Blake, ed. G. Keynes, 3 vols., Nonesuch Press, London, 1925.
Blake: Complete Writings, ed. G. Keynes, Nonesuch Press, London, 1957.
Blake: Complete Writings, ed. G. Keynes, a reprint by Oxford University Press of the 1957 Nonesuch edition, London, 1966. Available in both hardback and paperback. This is the best edition for students to buy.
The Poetry and Prose of William Blake, ed. D. V. Erdman, commentary by H. Bloom, New York, 1965.

BIBLIOGRAPHIES

G. Keynes, *Bibliography of William Blake*, New York, 1921.
G. Keynes and E. Wolf, *William Blake's Illuminated Books: A Census*, New York, 1953.
G. E. Bentley, Jr. and M. K. Nurmi, *A Blake Bibliography*, University of Minnesota, Minneapolis, 1964.
G. E. Bentley, *Blake Records*, Oxford, 1969.

SOME CRITICAL AND SCHOLARLY BOOKS ON BLAKE (in *addition* to those books from which extracts have been taken for *Critics on Blake*).

Hazard Adams, *A Reading of the Shorter Poems*, University of Washington Press, Seattle, 1963.

T. J. Altizer, *The New Apocalypse: The Radical Christian View of William Blake*, East Lansing, 1967.

John Beer, *Blake's Humanism*, Manchester University Press, Manchester, 1968.

—„—, *Blake's Visionary Universe*, Manchester University Press, Manchester, 1969.

Morchard Bishop, [Oliver Stoner], *Blake's Hayley*, London, 1951.

Bernard Blackstone, *English Blake*, Cambridge, 1949.

Jacques Blondel, *William Blake: émerveillement et profanation*, Paris, 1968.

Harold Bloom, *Blake's Apocalypse*, Victor Gollancz, London, 1963.

Jacob Bronowski, *William Blake 1757–1827: A Man Without a Mask*, London, 1943.

Martin Butlin, *William Blake*, (Tate Gallery Little Book Series), London, 1966, with plates.

S. Foster Damon, *A Blake Dictionary: The Ideas and Symbols of William Blake*, Brown University Press, Providence, R. I., 1965.

Northrop Frye, *Fearful Symmetry: A Study of William Blake*, Princeton, 1947, Beacon Paperback, 1962.

S. Gardner, *Blake*, (Literature in Perspective Series), Evans Bros., London, 1968.

D. G. Gillham, *Blake's Contrary States: The Songs of Innocence and Experience as Dramatic Poems*, Cambridge, 1966.

R. F. Gleckner, *The Piper and the Bard*, Wayne State University Press, Detroit, 1959.

Jean H. Hagstrum, *William Blake, Poet and Painter, An Introduction to the Illustrated Verse*, Chicago, 1964.

E. D. Hirsch, *Innocence and Experience: An Introduction to Blake*, New Haven, 1964.

C. J. Holloway, *Blake: The Lyric Poetry*, (Studies in English Literature Series), Edward Arnold, London, 1968.

W. R. Hughes, (ed.), *Jerusalem: A Simplified Version, With a Commentary and Notes*, London, 1964.

G. Keynes, *A Study of the Illuminated Books of William Blake*, Methuen and Trianon Press, London and Paris, 1965.

R. G. Lister, *William Blake: An Introduction to the Man and His Work*, London, 1968.

M. R. Lowery, *Windows of the Morning: A Critical Study of William Blake's 'Poetical Sketches', 1783*, Yale University Press, New Haven and London, 1940.

K. Raine, *Blake and Tradition*, 2 vols, London, 1969.

A. H. Rosenfeld (ed.) *William Blake: Essays for S. F. Damon*, Providence, R. I., 1969.

Joseph Wicksteed, *William Blake's 'Jerusalem'*, Trianon Press, London, 1954.

Mona Wilson. *Life of Blake*, Nonesuch Press, London, 1927, 3rd edition, 1948.

SOME USEFUL ESSAYS AND ARTICLES (in *addition* to those selected for *Critics on Blake*).

A. F. Blunt, 'Blake's Pictorial Imagination', *Journal of Warburg and Courtauld Institutes*, VI, 1943, pp. 190–212.

S. F. Bolt, 'William Blake: *Songs of Innocence*', *Politics and Letters*, I, 1947, pp. 9–14.

Vincent Buckley, 'Blake's Originality', *Melbourne Critical Review*, 7, 1964, pp. 3–21.

David V. Erdman, 'Blake: The Historical Approach', *English Institute Essays*, 1950, ed. Alan S. Downer, New York, 1951, pp. 197–223.

'Terrible Blake in his Pride: An Essay on *The Everlasting Gospel*', *From Sensibility to Romanticism*, 28, pp. 331-56.

Northrop Frye, 'Poetry and Design in William Blake', *Journal of Aesthetics and Art Criticism*, X, 1951, pp. 35–42.

'Blake's Introduction to Experience', *Huntingdon Library Quarterly*, XXI, 1957, pp. 56–67.

'Notes for a Commentary on *Milton*', *The Divine Vision*, ed. V. de S. Pinto, 1957, pp. 97–137.

R. F. Gleckner, 'Blake's Religion of the Imagination', *JAAC*, X, 1951, pp. 35–42.

'William Blake and "The Human Abstract"', *PMLA*, LXXVI, 1961, pp. 373–9.

'Blake and the Senses', *Studies in Romanticism*, V, 1965, pp. 1–15.

'Blake's Seasons', *Studies in English Literature: 1500-1900*, V, 1965, pp. 533–51.

Jean H. Hagstrum, 'The Wrath of the Lamb: A Study of William Blake's Conversion', *From Sensibility to Romanticism*, 28, pp. 311–30.

F. Kaplan, ' "The Tyger" and its Maker: Blake's Vision of Art and the Artist', *SEL: 1500–1900*, VII, 1967, pp. 617–27.

G. Keynes, 'On Editing Blake', *English Studies Today*, 3rd Series, 1964.

Karl Kiralis, 'The Theme and Structure of William Blake's *Jerusalem*', *ELH*, XXIII, 1956, pp. 127–43; reprinted in *The Divine Vision*, ed. Pinto, London, 1957, pp. 139–62.

Leo Kirschbaum, 'Blake's "The Fly"', *Essays in Criticism*, XI, 1961, pp. 154–62.

F. R. Leavis, 'Thought and Emotional Quality: Notes in the Analysis of Poetry', *Scrutiny*, XIII, 1945, pp. 53–71.

Wolf Mankowitz, 'William Blake: *Songs of Experience*', *Politics and Letters*, I, 1947, pp. 15–23.

H. M. Margoliouth, 'Notes on Blake', *Review of English Studies*, XXIV, 1948, pp. 303–16.

Josephine Miles, 'The Language of William Blake', *English Institute Essays*, 1950, ed. Downer, New York, 1951, pp. 141–69; repr. in *Eras and Modes in English Poetry*, Berkeley and Los Angeles, 1957.

M. K. Nurmi, 'Blake's Revisions of "The Tyger"', *PMLA*, LXXI, 1956, pp. 669–85.

Morton D. Paley, 'Tyger of Wrath', *PMLA*, LXXXI, 1966, pp. 540–51.

E. J. Rose, ' "Mental Forms Creating": Fourfold Vision and the Poet as Prophet in Blake's Designs and Verse', *JAAC*, XXIII, 1964, pp. 173–83.

'The Symbol of the Opened Center and Poetic Theory in Blake's *Jerusalem*', *SEL: 1500–1900*, V, 1965, pp. 587–606.

Ruthven Todd, 'William Blake and the Eighteenth–Century Mythologists', *Tracks in the Snow*, London, 1946, pp. 29–60.

T. P. Wolfe, 'The Blakean Intellect', *Hudson Review*, XX, 1967–8, pp. 610–14.